William E. Arnold

Summer in the Winter Time

William E. Arnold

Summer in the Winter Time

ISBN/EAN: 9783337258405

Printed in Europe, USA, Canada, Australia, Japan

Cover: Foto ©Andreas Hilbeck / pixelio.de

More available books at **www.hansebooks.com**

PRICE 25 CENTS.

Summer in the Winter Time

OCEAN STEAMSHIP COMPANY.
"THE SAVANNAH LINE."
SAVANNAH. NEW YORK. BOSTON. PHILADELPHIA.
1891-92.

TWILIGHT ON THE SAVANNAH RIVER.

"When the winter breezes blow
I generally go—SOUTH."
After H. M. S. Pinafore.

Summer in the Winter Time.

COMPILED BY
W. E. ARNOLD.

CAUTION. This book is fully covered by copyrights, and all rights reserved. All persons are warned not to use the information or any part thereof in other compilations or publications.

ISSUED BY PASSENGER DEPARTMENT
OF THE
OCEAN STEAMSHIP COMPANY,
"THE SAVANNAH LINE."

SAVANNAH.   NEW YORK.   BOSTON.   PHILADELPHIA.

1891-92.

Entered, according to the act of Congress, in the year 1891,

By W. E. ARNOLD,

at the office of the Librarian of Congress, Washington, D. C.

NOTE FROM THE COMPILER.

To our Southern Friends:

The information contained in "Summer in the Winter Time" is taken from data received direct from residents of the localities described, and in some cases received only after several requests for such information. In most instances the information has been freely and fully given, and the tender of assistance in the work has been so warmly expressed, that we feel greatly indebted for the proffer.

It may be that some will think we have not said enough about certain localities, and too much about others; if so, we plead the use only of "official" information—in some cases very meagre, and in others too voluminous to reprint in full; yet we have tried to use such, stating the salient points.

IMPORTANT.—That our next edition may be more complete, we ask our Southern friends to criticise this work carefully and freely, and call our attention to anything needing correction, reduction, or addition. Every criticism shall receive careful consideration. Of course, we all appreciate that we want to give all the "facts in the case," but want to put them as **briefly and tersely as possible.**

W. E. ARNOLD,
Compiler.

ADDRESS, { *July to March*—New Pier 35, North River, New York.
{ *March to July*—71 W. Bay Street, Jacksonville, Fla.

Richmond & Danville Railroad Co.,

Operating Steamship Lines of CENTRAL R. R. AND BANKING CO. of Georgia.

JOHN H. INMAN, President, 80 Broadway, N. Y.   W. H. GREEN, General Manager, Atlanta, Ga.
A. B. ANDREWS, Vice-President, Raleigh, N. C.   SOL. HAAS, Traffic Manager, Atlanta, Ga.
J. A. RUTHERFURD, Vice-Pres., 80 Broadway, N.Y.   J. M. CULP, Assistant Traffic Manager.
JAS. L. TAYLOR, General Passenger Agent, Atlanta, Ga.

"THE SAVANNAH LINE."

OCEAN STEAMSHIP COMPANY

(Between New York and Savannah, and between Philadelphia and Savannah.)

NEW ENGLAND & SAVANNAH STEAMSHIP COMPANY

(Between Boston and Savannah.)

C. M. SORREL, Manager,
SAVANNAH, GA.   NEW YORK.

R. L. WALKER, Agent, New Pier 35, N. River, New York.
RICHARDSON & BARNARD, Agents, Lewis Wharf, Boston, Mass.
C. G. ANDERSON, Agent, Savannah, Ga.
W. L. JAMES, Agent, 13 South Third Street, Philadelphia.

W. E. ARNOLD, Gen'l Traveling Pass'r Agent,
New Pier 35, N. R., New York.   71 West Bay St., Jacksonville, Fla.
(July to March.)   (March to July.)

W. H. RHETT, General Agent C. R. R., 317 Broadway, New York.
A. DeW. SAMPSON, General Agent C. R. R., 306 Washington St., Boston, Mass.
J. D. HASHAGEN, Eastern Agent S. F. & W. Ry., 261 Broadway, New York.
CARROLL H. SMITH, Eastern Agent S. A. & M. Ry., 379 Broadway, New York.
B. R. PRICE, General Agent, 71 W. Bay Street, Jacksonville, Fla.
W. H. LUCAS, Florida Passenger Agent, 71 W. Bay St., Jacksonville, Fla.
FELIX GARCIA, Traveling Passenger Agent, 71 West Bay St., Jacksonville, Fla.
S. E. P. DAVIS, Passenger Agent, New Pier 35, North River, New York.

3 LINES   The Finest and Fleetest Passenger Steamships flying the American Flag.   **3 LINES**

THE NEW YORK LINE

Has four steamers both ways each week leaving New York and Savannah every Monday, Wednesday, Friday, and Saturday.

THE BOSTON LINE

Has steamers leaving both Boston and Savannah every four days.

THE PHILADELPHIA LINE

FOR FREIGHT ONLY. (Passengers booked via New York.) Steamer leaves Philadelphia and Savannah every ten days.

Always Travel via The Savannah Line.

Do You?

Do you want health, comfort, ease, pleasure, sport, or sight-seeing? Do you wish to avoid disagreeable winter weather? IF YOU DO, GO SOUTH

Do you want a comfortable, inexpensive trip? Step into your nearest ticket office and purchase a through or excursion ticket, via THE SAVANNAH LINE, either from or via New York or Boston. Steamers leave New York every Monday, Wednesday, Friday, and Saturday; leave Boston every four days.

What do you want to see most? Make up your mind what will be most enjoyable, or most suitable to your taste or means. This book will tell you where it is.

Do you wish to visit the oldest town in the United States, with its relics of mediæval antiquity? This book will tell you where it is.

Do you want the finest hotels in the world, with the most luxurious appointments? This book tells of such.

Do you want a quiet spot where one can live at little cost? This book tells you of quiet, inexpensive places; of gay and fashionable places; of places varying in prices from $3 to $100 per week: surely, one can be suited.

Do you want "great sport" at hunting and fishing? This book will tell you where to go for both or either.

Do you want surf bathing, sailing, or boating? This book tells where they can be found.

Do you admire and enjoy curiosities of nature? This book tells of caves, sinks, boiling springs, wooded hammocks of wonderfully luxuriant growth, springs of water of unusual clearness and depth, and other wonderful things.

Do you want to see the finest of orange, lemon, pineapple, or cocoanut groves, large sugar, cotton, or rice plantations? They are in the section covered by this book.

To go South without visiting Savannah, is omitting a most important item of a Southern trip.

THE SAVANNAH LINE STEAMERS ARE THE FINEST.

THE CITY OF SAVANNAH.

This beautiful Southern city, with its wide, shaded streets, its beautiful parks, its pleasant homes, delightful drives, and its spacious modern hotels, is well worth many days travel merely to see. One is amply repaid such a trip; and for any one going South, without spending at least a few days in Savannah, there is an omission in the trip which will always be regretted.

Savannah is one of the oldest cities in the "States," settled in 1733; has a record, during the Revolutionary days, of which every Savannahian is proud, as evinced by the Greene Monument, the Jasper Monument, and the Pulaski Monument.

To the Northerner, Savannah has peculiar attractions—all pronouncing it "That Beautiful City." The drive to Thunderbolt, over the shell road, passing Cathedral Cemetery, Bonaventure, and Greenwich Park, with glimpses of Thunderbolt River, is very pleasant. And then a visit should be paid to see the beauties of Bonaventure, one of the most naturally attractive spots in this whole country, with its mighty yet graceful oaks, with their beautiful drapery of Spanish moss spreading their boughs and superb foliage over the wide avenues. While Bonaventure alone is sufficient to induce a visit to Savannah, there are, besides, many other attractive spots, among which may be noted Thunderbolt, Greenwich Park, Tybee Beach, Isle of Hope, Montgomery, Beaulieu, and White Bluff, all having their special claims.

Throughout the city are numerous lovely parks and spacious public squares, bordered by stately private residences and other imposing buildings. One of the finest and most complete hotels in the United States is located here. This attractive "Forest City" may equally well be called "The Monumental City." Its memorials to heroes, linked with its history from the hour of the city's birth on the lofty bluff amid the friendly Yamacraws, mark a grateful people. Greene, Pulaski, Jasper, and Gordon still stand before their eyes in stone and brass. The Confederate soldier, with his comrades fallen at Gettysburg, is commemorated by affecting and appropriate monumental art.

A native Canadian, who has recently visited Savannah, upon being pressed for an opinion, says: "I am a Canadian, and consequently have attended Canadian (not American) collegiate institutes where the history of our own and mother countries has been taught, and all historical facts connected with our Southern neighbors overlooked. I cannot, therefore, say anything (original) suitable for publication on such an historical city as Savannah; but, between ourselves, I must say I was delighted, in the fullest sense of the word, with the city, the De Soto, &c. O! do not overlook the cemetery: it is well worth a visit, and, without doubt, one of the finest sights in the world."

The Telfair Academy of Arts and Sciences, Telfair Place, Barnard, between State and President; open daily 10 A. M. until 5 P. M. Admission, 25 cents.

Georgia Historical Society, Whitaker and Gaston; open to members and non residents. Library hours 10 A. M. to 9 P. M.

The great wharves and docks of the Savannah Line are all easy of access by a complete system of electric street cars.

The office of the Ocean Steamship Company, "The Savannah Line," is at No. 3 Waldburg Building, at foot of Bull Street. C. G. Anderson is the agent.

TICKETS INCLUDE MEALS AND BERTH.

SAVANNAH, GA.

SPECIAL CONSIDERATIONS IN MAKING A TRIP SOUTH.

Any ticket agent can sell you a through or excursion ticket to any point in Florida or South via **The Savannah Line.**

The fares between the East and South to the two great distributing points—Savannah and Jacksonville—are:—

Rates.

From NEW YORK To SAVANNAH, Ga.	First Class Excursion Intermediate Steerage	$20.00 32.00 15.00 10.00
From NEW YORK To JACKSONVILLE, Fla.	First Class Excursion Intermediate Steerage	$25.00 43.30 19.00 12.50
From BOSTON* To SAVANNAH, Ga.	First Class Excursion Intermediate Steerage	$22.00 36.00 17.00 11.75
From BOSTON* To JACKSONVILLE, Fla.	First Class Excursion Intermediate Steerage	$27.00 47.30 21.00 14.25

* These rates from Boston apply via the direct steamers from Boston or via the New York line.

See your nearest ticket agent.

The price of through tickets is liable to change at any time, hence it is best to see your nearest ticket agent, or write to one of the agents named on page 6, to ascertain the rates in effect at the time. A call on your nearest ticket agent is always preferable. Talk the matter over with him. If he hasn't full data at hand, his experience in such matters directs him where and how to get full, complete, and reliable information in detail. He will engage state-room or berth on steamer, sell you a through ticket at the very lowest rate obtainable, check your baggage through, and relieve you of many details. Tell the

THE FASTEST PASSENGER STEAMSHIPS

SUMMER IN THE WINTER TIME.   11

Tickets including meals and berth. ticket agent you wish to go via **The Savannah Line** of Steamers, because the purchase of a through ticket via that line includes meals and berth, and all the luxury of a first-class hotel without additional expense, affording

Comfort en route. ample time for meals; the cry "twenty minutes for dinner" is unheard; ample space in saloons and on promenades for relaxation, rest, comfort, and pleasure.

A delightful trip. A trip to Florida or any point South, via **The Savannah Line**, means a variety of travel, including, as it does, a short sea trip (48 to 60 hours) on the finest and fastest passenger steamships in the American Merchant Marine, and also a rail trip on lines second to none in equipment, speed, and safety.

Two routes. **The Savannah Line** has passenger steamers from both New York and Boston, and freight steamers from Philadelphia.

New York steamers. Steamers leave New York from New Piers 34 and 35, North River, foot of Canal and Spring Streets, four times each week (Mondays, Wednesdays, Fridays, and Saturdays) at 3 P. M.

Boston steamers. Sailing schedules. Steamers leave Boston from Lewis Wharf every four days at 3 P. M. Sailing schedules will be sent to any address any time, or regularly every month, if desired.

Baggage. One hundred and fifty pounds of baggage on whole tickets, and 75 on half tickets, will be checked free of charge.

Children. Children under five years of age, free; between five and twelve, half fare; over twelve, full fare.

Rail connections. The rail connections at Savannah are very complete and perfect; the Central R. R. of Georgia, with its connections, reaching directly all points in Georgia, Alabama, Louisiana, Mississippi, Tennessee, and the South-west generally. The Savannah, Florida & Western Railway (The Plant System) has direct trains to South-west Georgia and all through Florida.

FLYING THE AMERICAN FLAG.

THE ROUTE TO THE SOUTH VIA SAVANNAH.

That Savannah, Ga., is really the gate to that land where we find Summer in the Winter Time, will be seen by a glance at the map below. Once upon a time "all roads led to Rome;" so now all roads in the Summer Land lead to Savannah.

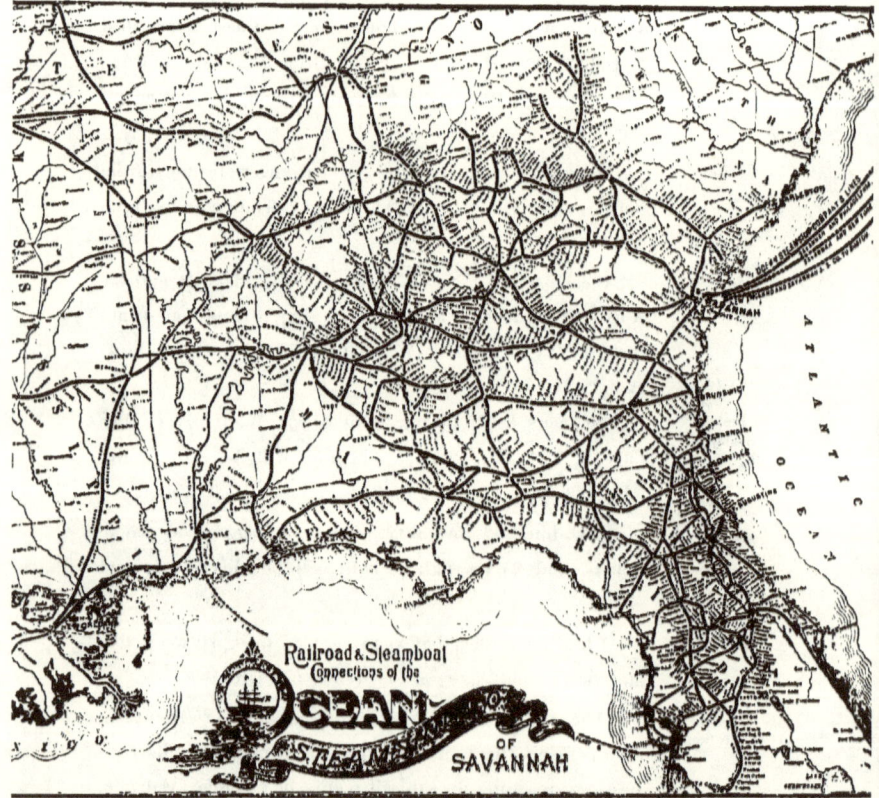

The very fact that "The Savannah Line" can profitably equip and maintain ten (10) of the **finest passenger steamships** in the American Merchant Marine, representing an aggregate tonnage of twenty-seven thousand four hundred tons, is substantial evidence that Savannah is the natural port to that section.

The Savannah Line is prepared to

SUMMER IN THE WINTER TIME. 13

The importance of Savannah's steamship service and connections may be instantly grasped by a few figures.

In the 12 months of the last business year there were 35 sailings per month of large coastwise steamers to New York, Boston, Philadelphia, and Baltimore, and as many arrivals from those ports, a total of more than 300 arrivals and departures each way per annum. This great fleet was, in the same period, supplemented by 101 large ocean steamers clearing direct from Savannah for foreign ports.

The steamships of **The Savannah Line** perform the service all the year: four ships each week from and to New York; one, every four days, from and to Boston; one, every ten days (for freight), from and to Philadelphia (Philadelphia passengers are booked via New York).

THE FLEET

Consists of the First-class Steamships

Kansas City, 4000 tons	Captain Kempton.
City of Birmingham, 3000 tons	" Burg.
City of Augusta, 3000 tons	" Catherine.
Tallahassee, 3000 tons	" Fisher.
Chattahoochee, 3000 tons	" Daggett.
Nacoochee, 3000 tons	" Smith.
City of Savannah, 2100 tons	" Savage.
City of Macon, 2100 tons	" Lewis.
Gate City, 2100 tons	" Googins.
Dessoug, 2100 tons	" Askins.

In the construction of these vessels no expense has been spared that would conduce to the

Comfort, Security, and Ease

of the traveler. The hulls and decks are of iron and steel. The staterooms contain two roomy berths each, and are much more commodious than the accommodations furnished in the finest foreign steamships.

The Table d'Hôte includes the delicacies of both the Northern and Southern Markets.

The officers or agents of the Company, named on page 6 of this book, will take pleasure in answering all inquirers desiring information as to passage or freight.

handle freight more promptly than others.

NAMES OF PLACES

IN THE

"Summer Land."

LOCATION, ATTRACTIONS, HOTELS AND BOARDING-HOUSES,
AND THEIR RATES.

Abbot (P. O. name **Hegman**), **Pasco Co., Florida.**—Station on Tampa Div., F. C. & P. R. R.; population of community, 300; telegraph and Southern Express Co.'s office; Dade City, 8 miles; good hunting and fishing.

Wm. Mote, Agent, F. C. & P. R. R.
Brack House.—E. H. Brack, Proprietor; L. P. Brack, Manager. Accommodates 50; $1 per day, $3.50 per week, $12.50 per month.

Aiken, Aiken Co., South Carolina.—On the South Carolina R. R., 17 miles from Augusta, Ga.; reached from Savannah via C. R. R. of Ga.; population, 3000; very popular winter resort; one of the prettiest towns in the South; splendid drives, ample livery.

Address "Chamber of Commerce" for information.
Highland Park Hotel.—B. P. Chatfield, Proprietor. Half mile from the station by carriage. Accommodates 300; $1 per day, $21 to $35 per week.
Park Avenue Hotel. -A. M. Taft, Proprietor. Fifty yards from the station. Accommodates 100; $2.50 per day, $12 to $18 per week.
Busch House. Henry Busch, Proprietor. Accommodates 40; near station; $2 per day, $10 to $14 per week.
Numerous private boarding-houses, at rate of $8 per week and upward.

Alachua, Alachua Co., Florida.—Station on the S., F. & W. Ry., 17 miles from Gainesville; population of the community about 200; in the midst of a hard timber and good farming country.

Williams House. F. E. Williams, Proprietor. Accommodates 20; $2 per day, $8 per week, $28 per month.
F. E. Williams will give information.

Alafia, Hillsboro Co., Florida.—Eight miles south of Plant City; population, 125; in the centre of one of the richest beds of pebble phosphate; several mineral springs near.

J. H. Frier will give information.

UNEQUALED FACILITIES.

Alamo, Gadsden Co., Florida.—Twelve miles from Quincy, which is nearest railroad station and money-order office, telegraph and express office.
  Address S. H. Strom for information.
  S. H. Strom.—Private board; 11 miles from railroad station by private conveyance. Accommodates 10; 75 cents per day, $3 per week, $10 to $12 per month.

Albany, Dougherty Co., Georgia.—Junction of Central R. R. of Ga., S. F. & W., and B. & W. Rys.; population, 5000; money-order post-office; Southern Express Co.'s office; telegraph and telephone; ample livery; artesian water; street cars; seat of Georgia Chautauqua Assembly.
  B. M. Comfort, Ticket Agent; John S. Clark, Freight Agent.
  Albany Inn.—Fields and Philpot, Proprietors. Accommodates 150; $2.50 to $3 per day, $12 to $16 per week, $45 to $60 per month; 4 blocks by street car or omnibus.
  Hotel Mayo.—Mrs. Z. T. Mayo, Proprietor. Accommodates 125; $2 per day, $10 per week, $30 per month; 3 blocks by street car or omnibus.

Albion, Levy Co., Florida.—Station on Cedar Key Division, F. C. & P. R. R.; population, 250; nearest telegraph, express, and money-order post-offices, Archer or Bronson; phosphate mines near.
  Albion House.—Mrs. Wm. Gowen, Proprietor. Accommodates 20; $2 per day, $10.50 per week, $30 per month.
  Wm. Gowen will give information.

Alliance, Jackson Co., Florida.—Eight miles from Cypress.
  J. L. Beauchamp will give information.

Altamonte Springs, Orange Co., Florida.—Station on S. F. R. R.; winter resort; clear-water lakes and orange groves; telegraph office; Southern Express Co.'s office; fishing, hunting, and boating.
  M. E. Brigham, Agent, S. F. R. R.
  The Altamonte.—The Altamonte Hotel Co., Proprietor; N. F. Priest, Manager. Accommodates 150; $4 per day, $17.50 to $25 per week; half mile from station by private horse car; livery; boats on lakes.

Alva, Lee Co., Florida.—On Caloosahatchie River, 80 miles from Punta Gorda; a community of 150; good fishing and hunting, deer, turkey, &c.; Myers is nearest money-order, telegraph, and Southern Express office, 17 miles distant.
  Hotel Nelson.—Peter Nelson, Proprietor. Accommodates 20; $1 per day, $5 per week, $20 per month.

Anclote, Hillsboro Co., Florida.—On the Gulf of Mexico, at the mouth of the Anclote River, 3 miles from Tarpon Springs; a community of about 15 families; good boating and fishing; 1½ miles from the anchorage of the Sponge Fleet.
  J. M. Craver or E. A. Hill will give information. Several private boarding-houses; $1 per day, $5 per week.

Anderson (P. O. name Andersonville), Sumter Co., Georgia.—Station on S. W. Division, Central R. R. of Georgia; population, 500; telegraph and Southern Express Co.'s office; National Cemetery. The stockade where Federal soldiers were imprisoned during the war is now being converted into a beautiful park by the G. A. R.
  W. M. Zirkle, Agent, Central R. R. of Ga.
  Wesson House.—Mrs. A. M. Wesson, Proprietor. Accommodates 30; $2 per day special rates by week or month; 75 yards from station.

SOUTHERN PRODUCTS TRANSPORTED PROMPTLY.

Anthony, Marion Co., Florida.—Station on Southern Division F. C. & P. R. R.; population, 300; money-order post-office; telegraph and Southern Express Co.'s office; good hunting; 2 churches; good school; vineyards, orange groves, and truck farms.

H. S. Smith, Agent, F. C. & P. R. R., or J. A. Pugh will give information.
The Standard Hotel.—Mrs. M. F. Pugh, Proprietor. Fifty yards from station; $2 per day, $7 per week, $25 per month.
Geo. Barker.—Private board.

Apopka, Orange Co., Florida.—Station on Florida Central and Peninsula R. R. and on Florida Midland Ry.; population, 500; 900 persons get mail at post-office; money-order office; Southern Express office; telegraph; near Lake Apopka, second largest lake in the State; Clay spring, a beautiful natural spring, 3 miles distant; good hunting and fishing; hilly.

W. T. Berry, Agent, F. C. & P. R. R.
R. C. Waters, Agent, Florida Midland Railway.
Lake House.—G. W. Goode, Proprietor. Accommodates 40. (Winter House.)
Central Hotel.—H. H. Derby, Proprietor. One and one-half blocks from stations. Accommodates 20; $1.75 per day, $6 per week, $24 per month.
Scott House.—Mrs. J. P. Scott. Accommodates 20; $1.50 to $2 per day, special by week or month.
Morgan House.—Mrs. Morgan, Proprietor. Accommodates 25; $1.50 to $2 per day.

Arcadia, De Soto Co., Florida.—On the C. H. Division of the Florida Southern Ry.; population of the community, 2000; telegraph and Southern Express Co.'s offices.

The Arcadia Hotel.—Ten rods from station; will accommodate 100.

Armstrong, St. John's Co., Florida.—Station on J., St. A. & H. R. R.

M. Lopez.—Private boarding-house, one-quarter mile from the station. Accommodates 10; $1 per day, $1 per week, $14 per month.
James Masters will give information.

Astatula, Lake Co., Florida.—On Little Lake Harris; Tavares, 9 miles distant, is nearest money-order post-office, telegraph and Southern Express Co.'s office; high; healthy; beautiful lake; fishing and hunting.

J. S. Kimball.—Private board; one-half mile from landing and station. Accommodates 20; $1.50 per day, $7.00 per week, $25 per month.
J. S. Kimball will give information.

Astor, Lake Co., Florida.—Station on St. J. & L. E. Div., Florida Southern Ry., also landing on St. John's River; population, 100; telegraph office; Southern Express Co.'s office; fine hunting and fishing.

J. E. Jones, Agent, Florida Southern Ry.
Astor House.—F. J. Hinson, Proprietor. Accommodates 50; $2 per day, $10 per week, $30 per month; 100 feet from railway station or landing of steamer.
St. John's House.—M. L. Huntley, Proprietor. Accommodates 20; $1 to $2 per day. $4 per week and upwards.

ALWAYS TRAVEL VIA THE SAVANNAH LINE.

Atlanta, Fulton Co., Georgia.—Northern terminus of the main line of the C. R. R. of G.; general offices of the Richmond & Danville R. R. system operating miles of rail and steamship lines; population, 70,000; one of the livest cities in the Southern country, frequently called "The Chicago of the South;" 12 railroads centering there.

Kimball House, $2.50 to $5 per day.
Markham House, $2 to $4 per day.
The Layden, 198 Peach-Tree Street.—Mrs. A. J. Lowe. Five blocks from Union Depot. Accommodates 100; $2.50 to $3.50 per day, $12 to $17.50 per week; special rates by the month.
Grant House.—Three blocks from depot. Mrs. N. N. Archer, Proprietor; A. B. Walker Manager. Accommodates 80; $2 per day, $10 per week, $30 to $35 per month.
Willey House (private board).—M. L. Willey. Three minutes' walk from depot; accommodates 50; $1 to $2 per day, $7 to $10 per week, $30 to $50 per month.
The Bristol, 12 and 14 Lloyd Street.—B. E. Hudson. Accommodates 50; $1.50 per day, $5 to $7 per week, $20 to $25 per month.

Auburndale, Polk Co., Florida.—Station on the South Florida R. R.; population of town and neighborhood, 400; telegraph and Southern Express office; nearest money-order office at Lakeland; boating, bathing, fishing, and hunting; beautiful clear-water lakes.

McLain House.—Lewis H. McLain, Owner; A. S. Benedict, Manager. Accommodates 30; near the station; $2 per day, $6 per week.
L. C. Bowyer, Agent, S. F. R. R.

Aucilla, Jefferson Co., Florida.—Station on Western Div., F. C. & P. R. R.; population, 100; telegraph and Southern Express Co.'s office.

W. T. Elmore, Agent, F. C. & P. R. R.
Aucilla House.—Mrs. A. Wolf, Proprietor. Accommodates 12; $1.50 per day, $4.50 per week, $18 per month.

Augusta, Richmond Co., Georgia.—On the C. R. R. of Ga., 132 miles from Savannah; a beautiful Southern city of 40,000 inhabitants; famous for its wide, shaded streets; complete system of electric street railways, and all the modern conveniences of a city; beautiful government reservation, park, arsenal and barracks. Famous winter resort.

M. C. Jones, City Ticket Agent; **W. C. Gibbes,** Ticket Agent, Union Depot.
Hotel Bon Air.—Situated in Summerville, a suburb, on the heights (known as the Sand Hills); is a great winter hotel. C. A. Lindsley, Manager. First class in every particular; reached by electric railway or bus; accommodates 400; $4 per day and upward; special rates by the week or month.
The Arlington.—L. B. Pettyjohn, Proprietor. On Broad Street; accommodates 400; $2.50 to $4 per day, $12.50 to $25 per week, $35 to $75 per month.
Planters' Hotel.—M. H. Camp, Proprietor. On Broad Street; accommodates 100; $2 to $2.50 per day, $10 to $17.50 per week, $30 to $50 per month.
Augusta Hotel.—B. S. Doolittle, Proprietor. Accommodates 200; $2 per day, $10 to $15 per week, $30 to $60 per month.
Hillside (private board).—Miss E. I. Carmichael, Proprietor. Accommodates 15; $2 per day, $10 to $15 per week.
Smyser House.—J. T. Holman, Proprietor. Accommodates 40; $15 per week.
Heard House.—Mrs. Anna T. Heard, Proprietor. Accommodates 50.

Aurantia, Brevard Co., Florida.—Station on J., T. & K. W. Ry., 10 miles from Titusville.

Address **A. S. Dickinson** for information.

THE SAVANNAH LINE STEAMERS ARE THE FINEST.

AUGUSTA, GA.

Avoca, Hamilton Co., Florida.—On the G. S. & F. R. R.; population, 50.

J. R. Mock will give information.

Avon Park, De Soto Co., Florida.—Twenty miles from Fort Meade; telephone connection; population of the community about 300; good hunting and fishing.

O. M. Crosby, room 18, 99 Franklin St., New York, or Avon Park, Fla., will give information.
Hotel Herona.—Miss M. E. Whitney, Proprietor. By stage or hotel team from the station; accommodates 75; located on the bank of the lake; free boats for guests; $1 per day, $7 per week, $25 per month.

Bakersburg (P. O. at Pierson), Volusia Co., Florida.—Station on the J., T. & K. W. R. Ry., 4 miles from Seville.

Mead House.—Four hundred yards from the station. Dr. Mead, Proprietor. Accommodates 20; $1.50 per day, $5 to $8 per week.

Baldwin, Duval Co., Florida.—Junction of Southern and Western Divisions, F. C. & P. R. R.; 19 miles from Jacksonville; telegraph; Southern Express Co.'s office.

A. B. Clark, Agent, F. C. & P. R. R.
W. H. Duprey (private board).—$1.50 per day, $5 per week, $20 per month.

Barberville, Volusia Co., Florida. Station on J., T. & K. W. Ry.; population, 50; Seville 10 miles distant; Southern Express Co.'s office at Eldridge, 2 miles.

J. D. Barber, Agent, J., T. & K. W. R. R.
Barber's House.—J. D. Barber, Proprietor. Accommodates 10; $1.50 per day.

Barco, Levy Co., Florida. Twenty-four miles from Ocala, 18 miles from Bronson; 200 get mail at post-office.

J. S. Pedrick will give information.

Barnesville, Pike Co., Georgia. Station on the main stem of the C. R. R. of Ga.; population, 3000; location of the Gordon Institute.

J. O. Walker, Agent, C. R. R.
Matthew's Hotel.—C. D. Matthews, Proprietor. Fifty yards from the station; accommodates 75; $2 per day, $7 per week, $20 to $30 per month.

Bartow (county-seat), Polk Co., Florida.—Junction of the South Florida Ry. and the Charlotte Harbor Div. of the Florida Southern Ry.; population, 2000; money-order office; Southern Express Co.'s office; telegraph office; centre of the phosphate region of South Florida; 6 plants now in operation within 5 miles of Bartow; 5 churches; substantial brick college (Summerlin Institute); good hunting and fishing; Kissingen spring about 4 miles distant.

R. Gamble, Superintendent, Florida Southern Ry.; D. E. Freeman, Agent, S. F. R. R.;
J. G. Torrey, Agent, F. S. Ry.
Carpenter House.—J. A. Armstead, Proprietor. Half mile from the station by hack; accommodates 100; $2 to $3 per day, $10 to $15 per week, $40 to $60 per month.
Wright House.—J. C. Wright, Proprietor. Accommodates 50; $2 per day, $10 per week.
Orange Grove Hotel.—Ph. Dzialynski, Proprietor. Accommodates 50; $2 per day, $10 per week.
Bartow House.—B. C. Pate, Proprietor. Accommodates 30; $1.50 per day, $7 per week, $20 per month.

THE FASTEST PASSENGER STEAMSHIPS

Bartow Junction, Polk Co., Florida.—Junction of main line and Bartow Branch of South Florida R. R.; population, 20; telegraph; Southern Express Co.'s office; nearest money-order office, Bartow.
W. A. Wescott, Agent, S. F. R. R.
A. H. Zachry, $1 per day, $5 per week, $20 per month.

Bay City, Hernando Co., Florida.—Station on Pemberton Ferry Branch S. F. R. R.; Lacoochee River 100 yards from the station; good fishing; sulphur springs near by; population, 50; Southern Express Co.'s office at Macon, distance 4 miles; telegraph office at Pemberton, 5¼ miles.
J. P. McCall (private board). Three-quarter mile from the station; accommodates 12; $1.50 per day, $6 per week, $20 per month.

Bay Port, Hernando Co., Florida.—On Weekiwochee River and Gulf of Mexico; 17 miles from Brooksville; population, 30.
Address W. J. Parsons for information.
Garrason House.—J. N. Garrason, Proprietor. Accommodates 25; $1 per day, $7 per week, $25 per month.

Bay View (P. O. name Seven Oaks), Hillsboro Co., Florida.—Six miles from Clearwater and 14 miles from Port Tampa; population of the community about 100; location of one of the largest lemon groves, and one of the finest nurseries.
R. D. Hoyt will give information.
Bay View House.—James McMullen, Proprietor; Dr. Bethel McMullen, Manager. $1.50 to $2 per day.

Beauclere, Duval Co., Florida.—On St. John's River, 10 miles from Jacksonville.
N. D. A. Sawyer will give information.

Belknap, Bryant Co., Georgia.—Station on the main stem of the C. R. R. of Ga., 30 miles from Savannah; population of community, 250; telegraph office.
T. B. Moore, Agent, C. R. R. of Ga.
Moore House, Mikell House, Thompson House, Southwell House, at $1.50 to $2 per day.

Belleview, Marion Co., Florida.—Station on Southern Division, F. C. & P. R. R.; population, 250; money-order office; telegraph office; Southern Express Co.'s office.
S. B. Vining, Agent, F. C. & P. R. R.
City Hotel. W. H. Marsland, Proprietor. Accommodates 25; $1.50 per day, $7 per week.
Hotel Belleview.—H. Knight, Proprietor. Accommodates 50.

Belmont, Hamilton Co., Florida.—On the Suwanee River, 7 miles from Jasper; nearest express office and telegraph office, Genoa.
W. L. Peeples will give information.

Belmore, Clay Co., Florida.—(See **Wilderness.**)

Benedict, Marion Co., Florida.—Three miles from Reddick, Fla.; daily stage; population, 100; good school; church services; mail daily; orange groves.
Parkview Hotel.—Miss J. W. Hill, Proprietor. Accommodates 30; $1 per day, $4 to $7 per week; 3 miles from station by stage, or will send carriage upon notice.

FLYING THE AMERICAN FLAG.

Beresford, Volusia Co., Florida.—Station on the J., T. & K. W. Ry.; junction of the main line and De Land Branch; also, on Lake Beresford (St. John's River).
L. C. Branning, Agent, J., T. & K. W. R. R.

Birmingham, Jefferson Co., Alabama.—Situated in the midst of the coal and iron region of Alabama (frequently called the "Pittsburgh of the South"); terminus of the Central R. R. of Ga., on main line of Georgia Pacific Ry., at which point connection is made with all points west and north; population, 40,000; some of the largest and most successful iron furnaces, &c. in the world are located here; fine, large Union Depot.

Blackshear, Pierce Co., Georgia.—Station on the S., F. & W. Ry., direct from Savannah; population, 1000; money-order, telegraph, and Southern Express Co.'s offices; good and healthy locality; good farming country surrounding.
Brown House.—Mrs. Allen Brown, Proprietor. Near the station; accommodates 50; $2 per day, $5 to $7 per week, $15 to $25 per month.
McMillan House.—Mrs. Mary McMillan, Proprietor; W. L. McMillan, Manager. Near the station; accommodates 30; $2 per day, $5 per week, $16 per month.

Blanton, Pasco Co., Florida.—Station on Orange Belt Ry.; population, 50; Southern Express Co.'s office; nearest telegraph or money-order offices, Dade City or San Antonio.
Blocker House.—F. E. Blocker, Proprietor. Accommodates 10; $1 per day, $4 per week, $15 per month.
F. E. Blocker, Agent, O. B. Ry.

Bloomfield, Lake Co., Florida.—On the south side of Lake Harris; by steamer from Leesburg, and telephone connection with Leesburg; population of the community, 250; numerous fruit and vegetable farms; good hunting and fishing.
Geo. J. King will give information.
Howerton House.—Mrs. M. Howerton, Owner; Geo. J. King, Manager. Accommodates 20; $1.50 per day, $6 per week, $22 per month.
Warner House.—Miss Lydia Warner, Proprietor. Accommodates 25; $2 per day, $6 per week, $20 per month.

Blue Springs (same as **Juliette**), **Marion Co., Florida.**

Bluff Springs, Escambia Co., Florida.—On L. & N. R. R. and Escambia River; population, 500; telegraph; Southern Express Co.; rolling country; spring water.
H. D. Markley will give information.
King James Hotel.—J. A. Jellison, Proprietor. Accommodates 40; $1.50 per day, $4.50 per week, $16 per month.

Boardman, Marion Co., Florida.—On the F. S. Div. of the J., T. & K. W. system; population, 200; telegraph and Southern Express Co.'s offices.
C. Livers, Agent, Florida Southern Ry.

Bostwick, Putnam Co., Florida.—Station on J., T. & K. W. Ry.; telegraph; Southern Express Co. and money-order office at Palatka, 9 miles distant.
W. A. Crandall, Agent, J., T. & K. W. Ry.

The Savannah Line is prepared to

SUMMER IN THE WINTER TIME.   23

Bowling Green, De Soto Co., Florida—On the Charlotte Harbor Division, Florida Southern Ry.; population of community, 300 people; telegraph and Southern Express Co.'s office.

A. D. McKinney, Agent, F. S. Ry.
Bryant House. A. A. Bryant, Proprietor. Accommodates 30; $1.50 per day, $3 to $5 per week, $15 to $20 per month.

Braidentown, Manatee Co., Florida.—A landing on the south bank of the Manatee River, about 6 miles from its mouth; in the midst of a great vegetable and orange producing country; hunting and fishing; oysters and clams; shell mounds; old ruins; population of the community, 300; money-order and Southern Express Co.'s offices; nearest telegraph office, Tampa, 36 miles.

Address **A. T. Cornwell** or **C. P. Fuller** for information.
Carr's Restaurant and Hotel.—Accommodates 30; $1.50 to $3 per day, $12 per week, $40 per month.
Patten House.—W. C. Patten, Proprietor. Accommodates 25; $2 per day, $10 per week, $35 per month.
Duckwall House.—Mrs. S. J. Duckwall, Proprietor. Accommodates 15; $2 per day, $10 per week, $30 per month.

Brandon, Hillsboro Co., Florida.—Station on Tampa Division, F. C. & P. R. R.; Southern Express Co.; Seffner, 2¼ miles distant, is nearest money-order and telegraph office.

V. M. Brandon will give information.

Branford (or **New Branford**), **Suwanee Co., Florida.**—Station on S., F. & W. Ry., also on the Suwanee River; take S., F. & W. Ry. from Savannah, Ga. direct; population, 500; money-order office; Southern Express Co.; telegraph; good drives; boating, hunting, and fishing.

D. E. Horn or **Ivey Bros. & Co.** will give information.
Branford House.—Mrs. J. H. Horn, Proprietor. Accommodates 20; $2 to $3 per day, $7 to $10 per week, $20 per month.

Bristol, Liberty Co., Florida.—On the east bank of the Apalachicola River; nearest railroad station, River Junction, 20 miles; population of the community about 500.

John D. McAliley will give information.
C. W. Blunt.—Private boarding-house; one-half mile from the landing.

Bridgeport, Putnam Co., Florida.—Landing on St. John's River; nearest railway station and telegraph office, Bostwick. 4 miles.

V. B. Webb or **Jacob Hochstrasser.**—Private boarding-houses.
J. A. Boughton will give information.

Bronson (county-seat), **Levy Co., Florida.**—Station on Cedar Key Division, F. C. & P. R. R.; near Gulf Hammock; good hunting; large and small game.

T. W. Shands, Agent, F. C. & P. R. R.
Oak Grove Hotel. Mrs. M. J. Quell, Proprietor. Accommodates 25; $2 per day, $7 per week, $18 to $22 per month.

handle freight more promptly than others.

Brooksville, Hernando Co., Florida.—Station on the Florida Southern Ry.; population, 600; money-order, telegraph, and Southern Express Co.'s offices; high, rolling country, mostly rich hammock.

I. M. Cox, Agent, F. S. Ry.
W. E. Law will give information.
Hernando Hotel. W. J. Turner, Proprietor. One-half mile from station by free bus; accommodates 75; $2.50 per day, $8 to $14 per week.
Central Hotel.—Mrs. C. M. Nevitt, Proprietor. Accommodates 30; free bus; $2 per day, special by the week or month.
And numerous boarding-houses, at $3.50 to $5 per week.

Brunswick, Glynn Co., Georgia.—Southern terminus of the B. & W. R. R. and E. T., V. & G. R. R.; reached from Savannah direct via S., F. & W. Ry. and Waycross or Jesup; population, 10,000; all the conveniences of a city; located on a bay near the Atlantic Ocean.

J. A. Montgomery, Ticket Agent, B. & W. R. R.
J. F. Norris, Ticket Agent, E. T., V. & G. R. R.
The Oglethorpe.—One block from the station; livery, telegraph, and other conveniences of a strictly first-class hotel; $4 per day.
Central Hotel.
Ocean House.
Scarlett House.—Mrs. F. L. Oakley, Proprietor, 204½ Bay Street. Accommodates 40; $1.50 per day, $7 per week, $25 per month.
Mrs. J. Swift.—Private board, 500 G Street; accommodates 25; reasonable rates.
G. M. Hay.—Private board; $1 per day, $5 to $3 per week, $20 to $25 per month.

Bryceville, Nassau Co., Florida.—Six miles north of Baldwin; population, 150.
Private boarding-houses, at $12 to $20 per month.
R. B. Brown will cheerfully give information.

Buffalo Bluff, Volusia Co., Florida.—Station on the J., T. & K. W. Ry.; population, 60.

Camilla, Mitchell Co., Georgia.—Station on the S., F. & W. Ry.; between Albany and Thomasville; population, 1100; money-order, telegraph, and Southern Express Co.'s office.

W. W. Collens, Agent, S., F. & W. Ry.
Hotel Georgia. W. A. Hurst, Proprietor. Accommodates 75; $2 per day, $8 per week, $25 per month. One-half mile from the station.
Daniel's House. Miss Janie Spence, Proprietor. $2 per day, $6 to $7 per week, $25 per month.
Mrs. J. Ellis.—Private board; $1 per day, $7 per week, $20 per month.

Campville, Alachua Co., Florida.—Station on the Southern Division, F. C. & P. R. R.; 100 people get mail at the post-office; nearest money-order office, Hawthorne, 5 miles.
J. A. Steele, Agent, F. C. & P. R. R.
Campville House. Mrs. Hall, Proprietor. Accommodates 15; $1 per day, $12 per month.

Candler, Marion Co., Florida.—Station on the Florida Southern Ry.; population, 225; Southern Express Co.'s office; telegraph office; nearest money-order post-office, Ocala, 15 miles.
H. W. O'Neil, Agent, F. S. Ry., or A. D. Moore, will give information.
D. C. Kennard. Private board. Accommodates 15; $1 per day, $5 per week, $20 per month; 100 yards from station.
M. M. Leigh.—Private board. Accommodates 20; $1 per day, $5 per week, $20 per month; 100 yards from station.

TICKETS INCLUDE MEALS AND BERTH.

Cedar Key (P. O. name **Cedar Keys**), **Levy Co., Florida.**—On the Gulf; the terminus of the C. K. Division of the F. C. & P. Ry.; population, 1200; money-order, telegraph, and Southern Express Co.'s office; fine bay for fishing and sailing; abundance of game near by.

R. M. Dozier, Agent, F. C. & P. Ry., or E. J. Lutterloh, Agent, Cedar Key Town Co., will give information.
Schlimer House.—N. Schlimer, Proprietor. Accommodates 40; $2 per day, $10 per week, $40 per month.
Bettelini House.—A. Bettelini, Proprietor. Accommodates 20; $2 per day, $10 per week, $30 per month.
Magnolia House.—I. H. Sutton, Proprietor. Accommodates 15; $1.50 per day, $5 per week, $15 per month.

Center Hill, Sumter Co., Florida.—Station on the Florida Southern Ry. Div. of the J., T. & K. W. system; population, 200; money-order, telegraph, and Southern Express Co.'s office; fine orange groves; good hunting and fishing.

R. C. Alworth, Agent, F. S. Ry.
Grand View Hotel.—G. P. Lovell & Son, Owners. Accommodates 40; one-quarter mile from the station.

Cerro Gordo, Holmes Co., Florida.—Landing on the Choctawhatchee; nearest railroad stations, Westville and Caryville, 6 miles; population, 700.

Cerro Gordo Hotel.—T. H. Pitman, five miles from the railroad station by mail buggy, and 30 yards from steamer landing. Accommodates 30; $1 per day, $5 per week, $12 per month.

Charlotte Harbor, De Soto Co., Florida.—On Charlotte Harbor Bay, 3 miles from Punta Gorda; population, 600; nearest money-order, Southern Express, and telegraph offices, Punta Gorda; good hunting, fishing, boating.

The Boca-Grande.—A. B. Sibley. $2 to $2.50 per day, $5 to $10 per week, $20 to $30 per month; near landing.
Charlotte Harbor Hotel.—Mrs. M. H. Curry. $2 to $2.50 per day, $5 to 10 per week, $20 to $30 per month; near landing.

Chaseville, Duval Co., Florida.—On the St. John's River, 7 miles from Jacksonville; population of the community about 300; nearest money-order, Southern Express, and telegraph offices at Jacksonville.

Dr. A. E. Tyng.—Private board; $1.50 per day, $10 per week.

Chattahoochee, Gadsden Co., Florida.—Same as River Junction; landing on the Chattahoochee River; station on the F. C. & P., S., F. & W., and P. & A. Railroads; population, 1000; money-order; Southern Express Co.'s office; telegraph office; hunting and fishing.

Jos. W. Albert, Agent, F. C. & P. and P. & A. Rds.
Riverside House.—J. W. Albert, Proprietor. Fifty yards from station; $2 per day, $7 per week, $20 per month.
Union Hotel.—H. Himson, Proprietor. Accommodates 30; 100 yards from station; $1 per day.

UNEQUALED FACILITIES.

Chipley, Harris Co., Georgia.—Station on the S. & W. Division of the C. R. R. of Georgia; population about 500; money-order, telegraph, and Southern Express Co.'s office; beautiful mountain scenery; near Pine Mountain; 5 miles from White Sulphur Springs; 12 miles from Warm Springs; in the midst of a fine agricultural and fruit country.
B. H. Maynard, Agent, C. R. R. of Ga.
Commercial Hotel.—H. C. McKigney, Proprietor. Near the station; accommodates 30; $1.50 to $2 per day, special by the week or month.
Pursell House.—O. T. Pursell, Proprietor. $1.50 to $2 per day, special by the week or month.

Chipley, Washington Co., Florida.—Station on the P. & A. R. R.; population, 800; money-order, Southern Express Co.'s, and telegraph office; good hunting and fishing.
Chipley Hotel.—E. N Dekle, Manager. Three blocks from station; accommodates 60; $2 per day, $7 to $10 per week, $20 to $30 per month.
Collier House.—Mrs. J. Collier, Proprietor. Accommodates 25; $2 per day, special rates by the week or month; 200 yards from station.
Numerous boarding-houses at $15 to $25 per month.

Chipola, Calhoun Co., Florida.—Twenty-two miles from Marianna.

Chuluota, Orange Co., Florida.—On Lake Mills, 6 miles from Oviedo; population of the community about 300; in the midst of high pine lands; good hunting and fishing; Lake Jesup, Indian River & Atlantic Ry. is now in course of construction.
Robert A. Mills will give information.
Appian-Way House.—Mrs. Emeline S. Swartley, Proprietor. $1 per day, $5 per week and upward.

Churchill, Marion Co., Florida.—On Lake Kerr; by boat to Norwalk Landing.
B. L. Hickman will give information.

Citra, Marion Co., Florida.—Station on the Florida Southern Ry. and Southern Div., F. C. & P. R. R.; a community of about 800 people; in the midst of orange groves; money-order office; Southern Express Co.'s office; telegraph office.
O. Hardgrave, Agent, Florida Southern Ry.
J. K. Van Sickle, Agent, F. C. & P. R. R.
Mrs. Pepper.—Private board; 200 yards from the station; accommodates 15; reasonable rates.

City Point, Brevard Co., Florida.—Landing on Indian River; nearest railway Station, Titusville.
A. L. Hatch, Agent, I. R. S. B. Co.

Clarcona, Orange Co., Florida.—Station on the F. M., also O. B. Ry.; nearest money-order, telegraph, and Southern Express Co.'s offices, Apopka, 4 miles.
L. A. Smith, Agent, F. M. Ry.
Warner House.—C. O. Warner, Proprietor. Accommodates 25; $2 per day, $10 per week, $32 per month; one-half mile from the station.

Clayton, Barbour Co., Alabama.—Station on the South-western Div., C. R. R. of Ga.; population, 1100; money-order post-office, telegraph and Southern Express Co.'s office.
S. Mabry, Agent, Central R. R. of Ga.
Enterprise Hotel.—W. F. Wright, Manager. Accommodates 50; $2 per day; near station.

SOUTHERN PRODUCTS TRANSPORTED PROMPTLY.

Clearwater Harbor, Hillsboro Co., Florida. On Gulf of Mexico, and Orange Belt Ry.; population, 300; money-order, telegraph, and Southern Express Co.'s offices.

J. Hope, Agent, Orange Belt R. R.
Orange Bluff Hotel.—A. T. Dulton, Proprietor. Accommodates 100; $3 to $4 per day.
Sea View Hotel.—Mr. Kamenski, Proprietor. Accommodates 40; $2 per day.
Commercial Hotel. Mrs. Scranton, Proprietor. Accommodates 30; $1.50 per day.

Clermont, Lake Co., Florida.—Station on the Orange Belt Ry. and the Tavares & Gulf R. R.; population of the community, 800; money-order, telegraph, and Southern Express Co.'s offices.

R. W. Hooks will give information.
Hotel Clermont.—J. T. Ellis, Proprietor. Fifty yards from the station. Accommodates 50; $2 per day, $10 per week, $30 per month.

Clio, Barbour Co., Alabama.—Station on the South-western Division of the C. R. R. of Ga.; population, 200; people in the community, 1500; Southern Express and telegraph offices; nearest money-order office, Clayton, 17 miles.

A. B. Stephens, Agent, C. R. R. of Ga.
McRae House.—Frank McRae, Proprietor. Half mile from the station by hack. Accommodates 25; $1 per day, $3 per week, $10 per month.

Cocoa, Brevard Co., Florida.—Landing on the Indian River; population of community, 300; Southern Express Co.'s office; telegraph office; near the headwaters of the St. John's River; boating, sailing, fishing, and hunting.

C. J. Schoonmaker, Agent, I. R. S. B. Co.
The Peck House.—Mrs. W. H. Peck. One hundred yards from the landing. Accommodates 20; $2.50 per day, $10 to $15 per week, $40 to $45 per month.
Delmonico Hotel.—Wm. Jarvis. Accommodates 20; $1 to $2.50 p r day.

Cocoanut Grove, Dade Co., Florida. On Biscayne Bay; nearest railroad station, Juno; population about 100; fine fishing and boating.

Biscayne House.—Chas. Peacock, Proprietor. Five hundred yards from steamer landing. Accommodates 50; $1.50 per day, $10 per week, $35 per month.

ALWAYS TRAVEL VIA THE SAVANNAH LINE.

Columbus, Muscogee Co., Georgia.—A station on the C. R. R. of Georgia, Columbus & Rome R. R., Columbus & Western R. R., and the Mobile & Girard R. R.; a pleasantly-located, enterprising, growing city; quite a manufacturing centre; the head of navigation on the Chattahoochee River; population, 20,000.

B. J. **Daniel**, Secretary Board of Trade, will cheerfully give information; also, J. C. Haile, Agent, C. R. R. of Ga.
Rankin House.—G. B. Day, Proprietor. One-fourth mile from the station by street car or hack. Accommodates 200; $2 to $4 per day, $18 to $30 per week, special by the month.
Central Hotel.—W. A. Daniel, Manager.
Vernon House.—E. A. Riddle & Son, Proprietors.
Brown House.—J. F. Bartlett, Proprietor.
Veranda House.—Mrs. C. B. Frazer, Proprietor.
Also numerous private boarding-houses, among which are:
Mrs. C. **Lary**, 21 W. Eleventh Street.
William M. **Griggs**, 204 Eleventh Street.
Mrs. Mary E. **Lyon**, 402 Eleventh Street.

Como.—(See **Lake Como.**)

Conant, Sumter Co., Florida.—On the Florida Southern Division of the J., T. & K. W. system; telegraph and Southern Express Co.'s offices.

G. **McLean**, Agent, Florida Southern Ry.

Conley (P. O. name **Daisy**), **Tatnall Co., Georgia.**—Station on the main stem of the C. R. R. of Georgia; population of the community about 100; the Conoochee River near by affords good fishing.

J. C. **Edwards**, Agent, C. R. R. of Ga.
Hotel La Echart.—P. Echart, Proprietor, fifty yards from the station. Accommodates 50; $1 per day, $5 per week and upward.

Cook's Hammock (same as **Steinhatchie**), **Lafayette Co., Florida.**

Courtney, Brevard Co., Florida.—Population, 300; landing on the Indian River; nearest railway station, Titusville.

E. P. **Porcher**, Agent, I. R. S. B. Co.

Crescent City, Putnam Co., Florida.—Located on Crescent Lake, a half mile from Crescent City Landing Station; population, 1000; money-order and Southern Express Co.'s offices.

W. H. **Preston** will give information.

Crescent City Landing Station.—On J., T. & K. W. Ry.; is the station for Crescent City; boat meets all trains.

Crown Point, Orange Co., Florida.—Station on the Orange Belt Ry., in the midst of fine orange and vegetable growing country; near Lake Apopka; population of community, 100; nearest money-order, telegraph, and Southern Express Co.'s offices, Oakland, 5 miles.

A. M. **Minor.**—Private boarding. Accommodates 20; $1.00 per day, $5.50 per week, $12 per month; 50 yards from station.
J. H. C. **Maguire**, Agent, O. B. Ry.

THE SAVANNAH LINE STEAMERS ARE THE FINEST.

Crystal River (or Crystal), Citrus Co., Florida.—At the head of Crystal River, and on the S. S., O. & G. R. R.; population of the community about 400; 15 miles from Dunnellon; fishing, hunting, oysters; only 8 miles from the Gulf.
W. S. Paul will give information.
The Riverside.—W. S. Paul, Proprietor.
The Willis House.—G. T. Willis, Proprietor. At rate $1.50 per day, $5 per week and upward.

Cutler, Dade Co., Florida.—On route from Key West to Miami, on the Atlantic Ocean.

Cypress, Jackson Co., Florida.—Station on the P. & A. R. R.; Marianna nearest Southern Express and telegraph office.

Dade City, Pasco Co., Florida.—Station on the F. C. & P. and South Florida Railroads; population of community, 1000; money-order office; Southern Express Co.'s office; telegraph office; in the Hill Country of South Florida.
J. F. Roberts, Agent, S. F. Ry.
D. T. Clement, Agent, F. C. & P. R. R.
Dade City Hotel.—J. A. Delcher, Proprietor. $2 per day, $10 per week, $30 per month.
Sunnyside Hotel.—Mrs. R. P. Nelson, Proprietor. $1.50 per day, $5 to $8 per week, $18 to $30 per month.
Davis House.—J. K. Davis, Proprietor. Accommodates 15; $1 per day, $5 per week, $20 per month.

Daisy, Tatnall Co., Georgia.—P. O. name for **Conley.**

Dallas, Marion Co., Florida.—Station on the F. C. & P. R. R.; 2 miles from Summerfield.
S. Smith will give information.

Davenport, Polk Co., Florida.—Station on the South Florida R. R.; population of the community, 50; telegraph office; the nearest money-order office, Kissimmee, 15 miles; nearest Southern Express Co.'s office, Haines City, 4 miles; good sport; large game—bear, deer, and turkeys.
C. G. Doby, Agent, S. F. R. R.

Dawson, Terrell Co., Georgia.—On the South-western Division of the C. R. R. of Georgia; population, 400; money-order office; telegraph and Southern Express Co.'s offices.
B. M. Wilson, Agent, C. R. R. of Ga.
The Farnum.—Mrs. B. M. Wilson, Proprietor. One-quarter mile from the station, in omnibus or carriage; accommodates 75; $2 per day, $10 per week, $30 per month.

Daytona, Volusia Co., Florida.—Station on the J., St. A. & H. R. Ry., also on the Halifax River; population, 1500; money-order, telegraph, and Southern Express Co.'s offices; fine boating, sailing, and fishing; Atlantic Ocean only 1 mile distant.
J. N. Treadwell, Agent, J., St. A. & H. R. Ry., will give information.
Ocean View House.—Parker & Trainer, Proprietors; W. H. Trainer, Manager. Accommodates 150; $3 to $4 per day, special by the week or month.
Fountain City House.—A. De Wilde, Proprietor. Summer address, Hillsdale, Bergen Co., N. J.; winter address, Daytona; $3 per day, $12 to $15 per week.
The Palmetto. Mrs. M. Hoag, Proprietor. $2 to $2.50 per day, special by the week or month.
Grand View Hotel.—Mrs. W. S. Herdman, Proprietor. Accommodates 150; $2 per day, special by the week or month.
Halifax House.—C. A. Longe, Proprietor. $1 to $1.50 per day, $5 to $8 per week.

TICKETS INCLUDE MEALS AND BERTH.

De Funiak Springs, Walton Co., Florida.—Station on the P. & A. R. R.; population, 100; Southern Express Co.'s and telegraph office.

Hotel Chautauqua; ; **Alabama Hotel; Cawthron House;** **Allegheny House; Crescent Cottage; Indiana House;** reasonable rates. West Florida Land Co. will give full information.

Dekle, Bradford Co., Florida.—Five miles from Lake Butler.

De Land, Volusia Co., Florida.— Population of the town, community and neighborhood, 2400; station on the J., T. & K. W. Ry., 6 miles from St. John's River; money-order, telegraph, and Southern Express Co.'s offices; all city conveniences, and very attractive in itself and its surroundings; seat of University; high, rolling pine land; numerous orange groves.

L. E. Spencer, Agent, J., T. & K. W. Ry.
Carrollton Hotel. G. A. Dreka, Proprietor.
Parceland Hotel.—M. H. Paree, Proprietor.
Floral Grove Hotel.—A. Seaman, Proprietor.
Waverly Hotel.—Mrs. Drake, Proprietor.
Hotel Putnam.—G. D. Gould, Proprietor.
Magnolia Hotel. Mrs. Swift, Proprietor.
Chandler House.—J. L. Chandler, Proprietor.
Pierson House.—M. Pierson, Proprietor.
City Hotel. W. B. Fudger & Co., Proprietors.
Olive Branch.—Mrs. Swift, Proprietor.
At rates of $2 per day and upward.
And numerous boarding-houses, at $1 per day, $6 per week, $20 per month and upward.

De Leon Springs, Volusia Co., Florida.—Station on the J., T. & K. W. Ry.; population of the community, 200; telegraph and Southern Express Co.'s office; formerly an old Spanish settlement; a boiling spring, sulphur water, discharging 50,000,000 gallons daily; beautiful forest.

J. H. Rothe, Agent, J., T. & K. W. Ry.
Berlin H. Wright will give information.
De Soto House.—H. C. Harpending, Proprietor. Three-quarter mile from the station by hack; $2 per day, $8 and upward per week.

Dellwood, Jackson Co., Florida.—Population, 300; near Marianna.
D. S. Burke will give information.
Coullette House.—J. P. Coullette, Proprietor. Accommodates 25; $1.50 per day, $8 per week, $20 per month.

Derby, Marion Co., Florida.—Eight miles from Santos; population, 60; Ocala, distant 10 miles, is nearest post-office; Southern Express Co.'s and telegraph offices.
J. H. Diefenbach will give information.

De Soto, Hillsboro Co., Florida.—On the west side of old Tampa Bay; population, 100; hotel in course of construction.
J. F. Blanton will give information.

Disston City, Hillsboro Co., Florida.—On Boca Ceiga Bay, mouth of Tampa Bay; 5 miles from St. Petersburg, which is the nearest money-order office; Southern Express Co.'s and telegraph offices.
R. L. Locke will give information.
E. J. Locke.—Private board; $1.50 to $2 per day, $10 per week, $25 per month.
G. Fripp.—Private board; $1.50 to $2 per day, $10 per week, $25 per month.

SOUTHERN PRODUCTS TRANSPORTED PROMPTLY.

BONAVENTURE, SAVANNAH, GA.

Dixon, Santa Rosa Co., Florida.—Seventeen miles from Miligan; population, 100.
  J. W. Baggett, Jr., will give information.

Dragem Junction.—(See St. Catharine.)

Drayton Island, Putnam Co., Florida.—On the St. John's River population, 60; nearest money-order office; Southern Express Co.'s and telegraph offices at Palatka, 35 miles.
  Dr. Pettitt.—Private board; one-half mile from the landing; accommodates 10; $8 per week.

Duette, Manatee Co., Florida.—On the Manatee River; nearest railroad station, Wauchula, 20 miles; population, 200.
  Laban Rawls will give information.

Dunedin, Hillsboro Co., Florida.—Station on the Orange Belt Ry., also on the Gulf of Mexico; population of the community, 200; money-order office; telegraph office; Southern Express Co.'s office; located on the banks of St. Joseph's Bay, which is 2 miles wide, affording excellent fishing, boating, and bathing.
  G. L. McClung, Agent, Orange Belt R. R.
  L. B. Skinner will give information.
  Arcadia House.—Henry Handy, Proprietor.
  Dunedin House.—Mrs. H. Beckert, Proprietor. Accommodates 60; $2 per day, $10 to $15 per week, $20 to $40 per month.

Dunnellon, Marion Co., Florida.—Station on the S. S., O. & G. R. R.; population of the community, 200; 25 miles from Ocala; telegraph office; in the midst of one of the largest phosphate districts in the State.
  Messrs. Leitner & Griner will give information.
  Renfro House.—W. W. Lindsay, Proprietor. Accommodates 20; $1.50 to $2 per day, $8 per week and upward.
  Griggs House.—S. L. Harding, Proprietor. Accommodates 20; $1.50 to $2 per day, $8 per week and upward.

Dupont, Clinch Co., Georgia.—Junction of main line and Gainesville Branch of S., F. & W. Ry., direct from Savannah; population, 750; splendid hunting and fishing; attractive locality.
  Suwannoochee House.—Dr. W. J. Nichols, Proprietor. $2 per day, $15 to $30 per month.

Eagle Lake, Polk Co., Florida.—Station on Bartow Branch, South Florida R. R.; population of community, 100; midst of beautiful lakes.
  W. H. Flowers, Agent, South Florida R. R., will give information.

Earleton, Alachua Co., Florida.—West side of Santa Fé Lake; by steamer from Waldo or Melrose; population of the community about 100; Santa Fé Lake is 20 miles in circumference; fine hunting and fishing.
  H. V. Noszky will give information.
  Private board at rates from $5 to $8 per week.

Earnestville, Pasco Co., Florida.—Near Abbott.

THE FASTEST PASSENGER STEAMSHIPS

Eastlake, Marion Co., Florida.—On the east shore of Lake Weir; station on the Florida Southern Ry.; situated on a bluff overlooking Lake Weir, a lake 6 miles long and 4 miles wide; population of the community about 100; Southern Express Co.'s office; nearest telegraph office at Weir Park; money-order office at South Lake Weir.

E. F. Carpenter will give information.
Eastlake House.—E. F. Carpenter, Proprietor. Summer address, Spencer, Mass. Accommodates 25; $2 per day, $8 to $10 per week.

Eau Gallie, Brevard Co., Florida.—Landing on the Indian River; population, 300; Southern Express Co.'s office; telegraph office.

J. H. Smith, Agent, I. R. Steamboat Co.
Trutter House.—Wm. Trutter, Proprietor. Near the landing; accommodates 50; $2 per day, $9 to $15 per week, $25 to $50 per month.

Eden, Brevard Co., Florida.—Landing on the Indian River; population, 175; great pineapple section.

T. E. Richards will give information.

Edwards, Gadsden Co., Florida.—Seven miles west of Quincy, and 4 miles from Mt. Pleasant; population of the community about 200.

Private boarding-houses, about $6 per week.
W. W. Edwards will give information.

Egleston Heights, Duval Co., Florida.—Station on the J., M. & P. Ry., 4½ miles from Jacksonville; seat of the Inskip Memorial Camp-Meeting and Chautauqua Society; to be the Ocean Grove of Florida.

O. H. P. Champlin will give information.
Hotel Egleston.—O. H. P. Champlin, Owner. Summer address, Ocean Grove, N. J. Frank & Adams, Managers. $1.50 to $2 per day, $8 to $10 per week, $25 to $30 per month.

Ehren, Pasco Co., Florida.—On O. B. Ry., 22 miles north of Tarpon Springs; population of community, 200; clear-water lakes; fishing and hunting; turkey.

W. A. Badgley will give information.
E. C. Cooper or Mrs. Tucker.—Private board; $1 per day, $3.50 per week.

Eldridge, Volusia Co., Florida.—Station on the J., T. & K. W. Ry.; population about 50; Southern Express Co.'s office; Pierson, distance 2 miles, is nearest telegraph office.

D. F. Morrison will give information.

Electra, Marion Co., Florida.—Near the Ocklawaha River; nearest railroad station, Weir Park, 7 miles distant; a community of 60.

J. C. Pillans will give information.

Ellaville, Madison Co., Florida.—On the Suwanee River; station on the Suwanee River Ry.; population, 350; money-order office; Southern Express Co.'s office; telegraph office.

W. R. Hines, Agent, F. C. & P. R. R.
Lester House.—Mrs. M. E. Lester, Proprietor. Accommodates 25; 150 yards from the station; $1.50 per day, $5 per week, $20 per month.

FLYING THE AMERICAN FLAG.

Ellenton, Manatee Co., Florida.—Head of navigation on the Manatee River; population of the community, 250; fine fishing and sailing; quail and other small game in abundance.
> E. B. Patton will give information.
> Private boarding-houses at rates of $1.50 per day, $6 per week and upward, by Mrs. Paddleford or Mrs. Nichols.

Ellerslie, Pasco Co., Florida.—Station on the Pemberton Ferry Branch of the South Florida R. R.; phosphate and kaolin near by.
> M. F. O'Neal, Agent, S. F. R. R.

Elzey, Levy Co., Florida.—Station on the Cedar Key Division of the F. C. & P. R. R.; population of the community, 500; money-order office at Bronson; Southern Express Co.'s and telegraph offices at Otter Creek, 2 miles distant.
> J. A. Williams, Agent, F. C. & P. R. R.
> Elzey House.—R. M. Elzey, Proprietor. Accommodates 15; $1 per day, $5 per week, $18 per month.

Emerson, Suwanee Co., Florida.—Nine miles from Branford; population of community, 100.
> A. J. Futch will give information.
> Futch House.—Mrs. A. J. Futch, Proprietor. Near; accommodates 25; $1 per day, $4 per week.

Emporia, Volusia Co., Florida.—One mile from Eldridge.
> W. T. Wasson or A. L. Baker will give information.
> Lake Hester Hotel.—A. L. Baker, Proprietor. One mile from the station; accommodates 50; $2 per day, $8 to $10 per week.

Enterprise, Volusia Co., Florida.—On Lake Monroe (St. John's River); station on the J., T. & K. W. Ry.; population, 500; money-order, telegraph, and Southern Express Co.'s offices; fine fishing and hunting; sulphur and salt springs; fine drives.
> F. L. Shaw, Agent, J., T. & K. W. Ry.
> Brock House.
> The Live Oak.—Mrs. T. Harold, Proprietor. Accommodates 20; $2 per day, $7 to $10 per week, $25 to $40 per month.

Esmeralda, Lake Co., Florida.—An island in Ocklawaha River, comprising 375 or 400 acres, all in orange groves.
> Mrs. M. L. Porter, P. M., will give information.

Estifenulga, Liberty Co., Florida.—On Apalachicola River, 35 miles from River Junction or Chattahoochee; population of community, 450; Southern Express Company's office; an attractive location in middle Florida.
> N. A. W. Eatsay will give information.

Etoniah, Putnam Co., Florida.—Four miles from Grandin; population of the community, 150.
> J. C. Strickland will give information.

TICKETS INCLUDE MEALS AND BERTH.

NATIVES.

Eucher Anna, Walton Co., Florida.—Five miles south of Argyle, which is the nearest telegraph and Southern Express Co.'s office.
C. Harrison will give information.

Eufaula, Barbour Co., Alabama.—On the South-western Division of the C. R. R. of Georgia; population, 6000; money-order office; telegraph office; Southern Express Co.'s offices.
A. H. Stevens, Agent, C. R. R. of Georgia.
St. Julian Hotel, G. L. Comer, Proprietor; and Arlington Hotel, John D. Godwin, Proprietor.—$2 per day, $10 per week, $25 per month.

Eureka, Marion Co., Florida.—On the Ocklawaha River; nearest railway station, Anthony, 15 miles, which is the nearest money-order, telegraph, and Southern Express Co.'s offices.
B. B. Barnum will give information.
R. A. Carlton (private boarding-house).—One-half mile from the landing; $1 per day, $6 per week, $12 per month.

Eustis, Lake Co., Florida.—Station on the Florida Southern Ry.; population of the community, 2000; money-order office; Southern Express Co.'s office; telegraph office; on the east shore of Lake Eustis.
Robert Taylor, Depot Agent, Florida Southern Ry.; B. F. Adams, City Agent, Florida Southern Ry., will give information.
The Eustis House; St. George Cottage; Ocklawaha House; Jackson House; Edward's Cottage, at rates from $1.50 to $2.50 per day, $6 to $12 per week, $25 to $45 per month.

Evinston, Marion Co., Florida.—On the F. S. Division of the J., T. & K. W. system; population, 200; telegraph and Southern Express Co.'s offices.

Exeter, Sumter Co., Florida.—Four miles south of Lake Harris and 15 miles from Leesburg.
L. G. Prescott will give information.
The Warren Sanitarium. Dr. Warren, of Boston, Mass., Physician and Manager; special rates.

Fairbanks, Alachua Co., Florida—On the Cedar Key Division of the F. C. & P. R. R.; population about 100; 7 miles from Gainesville, Fla.
C. H. Furman, Agent, F. C. & P. R. R.
McKibben's.—J. C. McKibben, Proprietor. $1.50 to $2 per day, $5 to $7 per week, $25 to $30 per month.

Farmdale, Calhoun Co., Florida.—Twenty miles from St. Andrew's Bay; population, 60; nearest railroad station, Chipley.
W. F. Woodford will give information.

Federal Hill, Clay Co., Florida.—On the St. John's River, also 5 miles south-west of Peoria Station, and 7 miles from Orange Park; small game; some deer; brook fishing.
Chas. D. Miller will give information.
Private board at $1 per day, $3.50 to $5 per week.

Federal Point, Putnam Co., Florida.—Landing on the St. John's River; population of the community about 250; fine fishing and boating; in the midst of many bearing orange groves.
J. F. Tenney will give information.
The Folsom.—Mrs. S. G. Folsom, Proprietor. $1 to $2 per day, $5 to $10 per week.

THE SAVANNAH LINE IS PREPARED TO

Fernandina, Nassau Co., Florida.—Sea-side terminus of the F. C. & P. R. R.; population, 3500; money-order, telegraph, and Southern Express Co.'s office.
E. D. Lukinbill, Agent, F. C. & P. R. R.
Among the hotels are "The Egmont," "The Florida House," and Mrs. F. R. Sweet's private boarding-house.

Figulus, Dade Co., Florida.—On Lake Worth; population, 200; nearest railway station, Titusville.
Cocoanut Grove House.—Near.

Five Points, Chambers Co., Alabama.—On the S. & W. Division of the C. R. R. of Ga.; population of the community about 250; telegraph and Southern Express Co.'s office; in the midst of a very productive and prosperous country.
Miss Ira Mooty, Agent, C. R. R. of Ga.
Smith House.—J. H. C. Smith, Proprietor. Accommodates 25; near the station; $1 per day, $4 per week and upward.

Floral Bluff, Duval Co., Florida.—Station on the J., M. & P. B. R. R.; 4 miles from Jacksonville.

Formosa, Orange Co., Florida.—On the South Florida R. R.; 2 miles north of Orlando.
F. E. Bosse.—Private board. From $1 per day and $6 per week upward.

Fort Fannin (P. O. name Fannin), Levy Co., Florida.—On the Suwanee River; 24 miles from Bronson.
J. C. McGrew will give information.
Mrs. McGrew. Private board. $1 per day, $5 per week, $18 per month.

Fort Gates, Putnam Co., Florida.—Landing on west side of St. John's River, opposite Fruitland, which is the post-office; 30 miles from Palatka; a settlement of winter residences and fine bearing orange groves.
J. Monroe Taylor will give information.

Fort Mason, Lake Co., Florida.—On the Florida Southern Ry., on Lake Eustis; population of the community about 600; Eustis, distant 2 miles, is nearest money-order, telegraph, and Southern Express Co.'s offices.
J. W. Lee will give information.
Lake View House.—D. W. King, Proprietor. Accommodates 50; 100 yards from the station; $2 per day, $7 to $10 per week, $20 to $30 per month.

Fort Meade, Polk Co., Florida.—Station on the C. H. Division of the Florida Southern Ry.; population, 400; money-order, telegraph, and Southern Express Co.'s office; telephone to Bartow and Avon Park; near Peace River; fine orange groves.
A. H. Adams, Postmaster, or L. E. White, Agent, Florida Southern Ry., will give information.
Adams House.—A. H. Adams, Proprietor. Three-quarter mile from the station by street-car line; $2 per day, $10 per week, special by the month.

Fort Myers (or Myers), Lee Co., Florida.—Nearest railway station, Punta Gorda; population, 300; money-order office. (See **Myers.**)

HANDLE FREIGHT MORE PROMPTLY THAN OTHERS.

Fort Ogden, De Soto Co., Florida.—Station on the Charlotte Harbor Division of the Florida Southern Ry.; phosphate works; fine orange groves near by; population of the community about 300; money-order, telegraph, and Southern Express Co.'s offices.

R. L. Haines, Agent, Florida Southern Ry.
Johnson House —W. A. Johnson, Proprietor. One hundred yards from the station; $1 to $2 per day, $5 to $10 per week.

Fort Reed, Orange Co., Florida.—Station on the Sanford & Indian River Division of the South Florida Ry.; population of the community, 250.

R. H. Whitner will give information.

Fort White, Columbia Co., Florida.—Station on the S., F. & W. Ry.; hunting, fishing, and plenty of quail; phosphate lands; 2 rivers near by; population, 500; money-order, telegraph, and Southern Express Co.'s offices; phosphate; good hunting and fishing.

Ruff House.—T. J. Ruff, Proprietor. Four hundred yards from the station; $2 per day, $10 per week, $30 per month.
Bardin House.—B. T. Bardin, Proprietor. One hundred yards from the station; $2 per day, $10 per week, $30 per month.
Weeks House.—H. M. Weeks, Proprietor. $1 to $1.50 per day, $5 per week, $20 per month.

Francis, Putnam Co., Florida.—Station on the Florida Southern Ry., 5 miles from Palatka.

J. H. Hickenlooper, Agent, Florida Southern Ry.
Mrs. C. Zeigler.—Private board; $3 per week, $12 per month.

Frankland, Alachua Co., Florida.—Twelve miles from High Springs.
David C. Beech will give information.

Fruit Cove, St. John's Co., Florida.—On the St. John's River; population of the community, 120.
William Peel will give information.

Fruitland, Putnam Co., Florida.—Landing on the St. John's River; population of the community about 100; nearest railroad station, Huntington, 6 miles.
S. R. Causey will give information.
Fruitland House.—Mrs. E. E. Austin; 200 yards from the landing; $2 per day, $10 per week, $30 per month.

Fruitland Park, Lake Co., Florida.—Station on the Florida Southern Ry.; high, rolling pine land; 20 clear-water lakes near by; population about 300; 4 miles from Leesburg.

W. A. Herring, Agent, Florida Southern Ry.
F. M. Buck or E. W. Kline.—Private boarding; one-fourth mile from the station; $1 to $1.50 per day, $5 to $7 per week, $20 to $25 per month.

Fulton, Duval Co., Florida.—Landing on the St. John's River, 12 miles from Jacksonville.
William Fisher will give information.

SOUTHERN PRODUCTS TRANSPORTED PROMPTLY.

Phosphate Mining.

Gabriella, Orange Co., Florida.—Station on the East Fla. & A. R. R., 6 miles east of Winter Park, and 5 miles from Oviedo; beautiful, rolling, high pine land; numerous clear-water lakes and young bearing orange groves.

Sherman Adams will give information.

Gainesville (county-seat), **Alachua Co., Florida.**—Station on the S., F. & W. and F. C. & P. Railroads; population, 5000; money-order, telegraph, and Southern Express Co.'s offices—in fact, all the conveniences of a city; the seat of the East Florida Seminary and State Military Institute; good fishing and hunting; good drives.

J. A. Goodwin, Ticket Agent, Florida Southern.
H. E. Day, Agent, F. C. & P. R. R.
W. P. Sheffield, Agent, S., F. & W. R. R.
Brown House.—Mrs. Starke, Proprietor; J. H. Graham, Manager. Accommodates 100; $2.50 to $3 per day, $12 to $18 per week, $40 to $60 per month.
White House.—Mrs. D. C. Adams, Proprietor. Accommodates 50; $2 to $2.50 per day, special by the week or month.

EAST FLORIDA SEMINARY, AT GAINESVILLE.

Gaiter, Marion Co., Florida.—Nine miles from Leroy; good fishing and hunting; deer and wild turkey.

J. H. McCoy will give information.
G. O. Turner or J. H. McCoy.—Private board at $4 per week and upward.

Georgetown, Quitman Co., Georgia.—On the South-western Division of the C. R. R. of Ga., 2 miles from Eufaula.

R. T. Gilbert, Agent, C. R. R. of Ga.
Mrs. Netty Lewis.—Private board; $1.50 per day, $7.50 per week, $25 per month.

Georgianna, Brevard Co., Florida.—Landing on the Indian River, 25 miles from Titusville; population about 200; 5 miles below Rockledge, and only a short distance to the ocean, with frequent communication ; good fishing, boating, and sailing.
F. C. Allen, Agent, I. R. S. B. Co.
Island Home Boarding-House.—Mrs. P. A. Black, Proprietor. $1.50 to $2 per day, $7 per week, $25 per month.

Geneva, Orange Co., Florida.—Located between lakes Harney and Jessup, 9 miles from Oviedo; population of community between 300 and 400; fishing; orange groves.
W. J. Brockton will give information.
Caldwell House.—G. F. Caldwell, Proprietor. $1.50 to $2 per day, $5 to $10 per week, $20 to $30 per month.

Glencoe, Volusia Co., Florida.—On A. & W. R. R.; population of community, 100.
C. R. Howard will give information.

Glen Ethel, Orange Co., Florida.—Station on the Orange Belt Ry.; rolling country ; clear-water lakes; Wekiva River for fishing and hunting.
C. A. Root will give information.
G. A. Michael.—Private board ; one-quarter mile from the station. Accommodates 25 ; $1 per day, $5 per week, special by the month.

Glen St. Mary, Baker Co., Florida.—Station on the Western Division of the F. C. & P. R. R.; population, 300; money-order, telegraph, and Southern Express Co.'s offices at McClenny, 2½ miles.

Glenwood, Volusia Co., Florida.—Station on the J., T. & K. W. Ry.; telegraph and Southern Express Co.'s offices; population of the community about 200; surrounded by several large orange groves.
S. J. Waits, Agent, J., T. & K. W. R. R.
Hotel Delano.—Mrs. W. B. Hall, Proprietor. Accommodates 30; one-quarter mile from the station; $1 per day, $5 per week and upward.

Goodwater, Coosa Co., Alabama.—Station on the S. & W. Division of the C. R. R. of Ga.; population, 1000; money-order, telegraph, and Southern Express Co.'s offices; fine schools ; 4 churches ; good drainage ; fine freestone water.
J. W. J. Targarson, Agent, C. R. R. of Ga.
Caldwell House.—A. Caldwell, Proprietor.
Pope House.—Mrs. C. M. Pope, Proprietor. $2 per day, $7 per week, $12.50 per month.

Graceville, Jackson Co., Florida.—Fourteen miles from Chipley.
G. B. Yawn will give information.
Private board: $1 per day, $4.50 per week, $15 per month.

Gracy, Alachua Co., Florida.—Four miles from Newnansville.
L. C. Gracy will give information.

Grand Island, Lake Co., Florida.—Station on the Florida Southern Ry.; 4 miles from Eustis; between Lakes Eustis and Yale; fishing, hunting.
J. M. Igou will give information.
The High Pines.—J. E. Wheelock, Proprietor. $1.50 per day, $7 per week, $25 per month.

The Savannah Line Steamers are the Finest.

Green Cove Springs, Clay Co., Florida.—Station on the J., T. & K. W. Ry.; landing on the St. John's River; money-order, telegraph, and Southern Express Co.'s office; population of the town and neighborhood about 3000; warm sulphur springs; bathing pools; parks; drives; good deer, turkey, and bird shooting; fishing and boating.

   T. J. Perkins, Agent, J., T. & K. W. Ry., or J. E. Low or Dr. J. W. Applegate will give information.
   Clarendon Hotel.—Harris & Applegate, Proprietors; Dr. J. W. Applegate, Manager. Two hundred yards from the station by street car; accommodates 200; $3.50 per day, $17.50 to $21 per week, special by the month.
   St. Elmo.—J. L. Scott, Proprietor.
   St. Clair.—T. T. Edgerton, Proprietor.
   The Oakland.—Mrs. A. Wiley, Proprietor. All reached by street cars or carriages.
   Numerous private boarding-houses, among which are the following:
   Riverside House.—D. F. Tyler, Proprietor.
   Spring Cottage.—Mrs. M. N. Moore, Proprietor.
   Glynn Cottage.—Mrs. D. J. Sallem, Proprietor.
   Howard Cottage.—Mrs. A. C. Lovelace, Proprietor.
   At rates of about $10 per week.

Greenland, Duval Co., Florida.—Station on the J., St. A. & H. R. R., near Jacksonville.

   A. Payne will give information.

Greenville, Madison Co., Florida.—On the Western Division of the F. C. & P. R. R.; population, 800; telegraph and Southern Express Co.'s offices; fine hunting and fishing; several fine yellow sulphur springs within short ride of the station.

   J. W. Hammerly, Agent, F. C. & P. R. R.
   Private board by Mrs. G. A. Cobb or W. D. Griffen: $1.50 per day, $7 per week, $20 per month and upward.

Greenwood, Jackson Co., Florida.—Nine miles from Marianna.

   A. B. Revely will give information.
   Mrs. G. C. Irwin (private board).—$1 per day.

Griswoldville, Jones Co., Georgia.—On the main stem of the C. R. R. of Georgia, 9 miles from Macon; one of the highest points on the Central R. R., between Macon and Savannah; supplied with freestone water.

   J. R. Van Buren, Agent, C. R. R. of Georgia.
   Liberty Lawn.—J. R. Van Buren, Proprietor. $2 per day, $10 per week, $35 per month.

Grove City, De Soto Co., Florida.—On Lemon Bay; nearest railroad station, Punta Gorda.

   G. H. Hafer will give information.
   Gulf House.—Gulf City Land Co., Proprietor. Accommodates 75; $2 per day, $10 per week, $30 per month.

Grove Park, Alachua Co., Florida.—Station on the Florida Southern R. R.; population, 100.

   W. G. Pogue, Agent, Florida Southern R. R.
   Sunnyside House.—Rev. N. G. Hawley, Proprietor.

Grover, Suwanee Co., Florida.—On Suwanee River, 11 miles from Live Oak.

   J. R. Melks will give information.

ALWAYS TRAVEL VIA THE SAVANNAH LINE.

Guerryton, Bullock Co., Alabama.—On the S. & W. Division of the C. R. R. of Ga.
G. E. Robinson, Agent, C. R. R. of Georgia.

Guilford, Bradford Co., Florida.—Six miles from Lake Butler.
Jacob G. Roberts will give information.

Gulf Hammock, Levy Co., Florida.—Nine miles from Otter Creek station; fine hunting for large game; fresh and salt water fishing.
C. B. Wingate will give information.
Gulf Hammock Hotel.—C. B. Wingate, Proprietor. $2 per day, $10 per week, $35 per month.

Hagen (P. O. name **Lulu**), **Columbia Co., Florida.**—On the G. S. & F. R. R.
R. C. Gillon will give information.

Haines City, Polk Co., Florida.—Station on the South Florida R. R.; population, 100; telegraph and Southern Express Co.'s office; boating, fishing, and hunting; turkey, quail, and bear.
A. B. Stroud, Agent, South Florida R. R.
Pine Grove Hotel.—Jules Lameraux, Proprietor. Fifty yards from the station. Accommodates 25; $2 per day, $5 per week, $20 per month.

Halcyondale, Screven Co., Georgia.—Station on the main stem of the C. R. R. of Georgia; population of the community about 150; telegraph and Southern Express Co.'s office.
W. H. Crawford, Agent, C. R. R. of Georgia.
Newton House.—D. J. Newton, Proprietor. One hundred yards from the station; accommodates 20; $2 per day, $15 to $20 per month.

Hamilton, Harris Co., Georgia.—On the S. & W. Division of the C. R. R. of Georgia; population, 750; money-order, telegraph, and Southern Express Co.'s office.
E. B. Gammel, Agent, C. R. R. of Georgia.
Hamilton Hotel, A. F. Truett, Proprietor, and the Turner House, Miss F. F. Turner, Proprietor.—$2 per day, $7 per week, $20 per month.

Hammock Ridge, Alachua Co., Florida.—Station on the Cedar Key Division of the F. C. & P. R. R.; the home of "The Harmony Club," who have a club-house which will accommodate 40 people (members only).
C. P. Perry will give information.

Hampton, Brevard Co., Florida.—Station on the Southern Division of the F. C. & P. R. R., also on the G. S. & F. R. R.; population, 300; telegraph and Southern Express Co.'s offices; 3 or 4 lakes within 4 miles, affording good fishing; also plenty of small game.
M. N. Blanton, Agent, F. C. & P. R. R.

Hardeeville, Brevard Co., Florida.—Landing on the Indian River; population of the community about 100; good hunting and fishing; deer, bear, and all kinds of birds in abundance; ducks on the river; hotel in course of construction.
W. W. Winthrop will give information.

Harlem, Putnam Co., Florida.—Six miles from Baywood; population of the community, 50.

THE FASTEST PASSENGER STEAMSHIPS

SUMMER IN THE WINTER TIME. 47

Harrison, Washington Co., Florida.—On St. Andrew's Bay; nearest railroad station, Chipley.
C. J. Demerest will give information.
New hotel to open September 1st. G. W. Jenks, Proprietor. $1 to $2.50 per day, $5 to $10 per week.

Hartland, Brevard Co., Florida.—Landing on the Indian River, 10 miles from Melbourne; population of the community, 100; good fishing and hunting.
J. C. Hart.—Private board. $2 per day, $6 per week and upward.

Haskell, Polk Co., Florida.—On the Pemberton Ferry Branch of the South Florida R. R.; numerous lakes.
T. A. Goode will give information.

Hatch's Bend, Lafayette Co., Florida.—On the Suwanee River. 6 miles from Branford; a community of about 150.
The Sims House.—J. B. Sims, Proprietor; 2 miles from the landing by hack. $2 per day, $5.50 per week, $20 per month.
J. B. Sims will give information.

Havana, Cuba.—Capital of the island and residence of the governor and all the state officials; population, 300,000; reached by the Plant S. S. Line; the steamships "Olivette" and "Mascotte," the greyhounds of the U. S. Marine Mail Service, leaving Port Tampa and Havana three times each week in the winter, and twice in summer, calling at Key West.

Passports are not necessary to visit Cuba; all that is necessary is a certificate, in due form, issued by any notary public, that one is an American citizen, giving residence; this is to be "*cised*" by the proper Cuban officer in order that one may be allowed to leave the island. These certificates can be obtained of ticket agents at Jacksonville, Sanford, Tampa, or Port Tampa, or from purser on Plant Steamers; the fee is $1; the fee in Cuba is 30 cents.

Visitors and tourists should have mail, &c. addressed, "Care Lawton Bros., bankers, and agents Plant S. S. Line, No. 35 Mercaderes Street, Havana, Cuba," who are Americans, and take pleasure in attending to such matters.

U. S. currency is taken at full market value by hotels, or Messrs. Lawton Bros. will exchange Spanish money therefor, allowing highest current rates.

Hotels and all parts of the city are reached by public cabs or coupés, which are very numerous, at low rates. The hotel interpreter meets all ships on arrival and attends to details.

Hotel Pasaje.—Manuel Linares, Proprietor. Accommodates 250; $4 to $6 per day.
Grand Hotel Roma.—John Repko, Proprietor. Accommodates 85; $3 to $3.50 per day, $14 to $17.50 per week.
Hotel Telegrafo.—F. Gonzalez & Co., Proprietors. Accommodates 100; $2 to $4 per day.
Grand Hotel Inglaterra.—Quan F. Villamil, Proprietor; Urbano Gonzalez, Manager. Accommodates 300; $3 to $6 per day, $20 to $40 per week, $85 to $170 per month.
Mascotte Hotel.—J. Carbonelle & Co., Proprietors. Accommodates 250; $2.50 to $4 per day.
Hotel Saratoga.—Mrs. Rosario de Aliart, Proprietor. Accommodates 48; $2 to $3 per day.
Hotel de Francia.—Peter Roig, Proprietor; Calderon, Manager. Accommodates 60; $1.50 to $2 per day, $45 to $60 per month.
Henry Fisher, 55 Havana Street.—Boarding-house; $2 per day, $51 per month.

FLYING THE AMERICAN FLAG.

Hawthorne, Alachua Co., Florida.—Station on the Florida Southern Ry. Division of the J., T. & K. W. system, also on the Southern Division of the F. C. & P. R. R.; population of the community, 600; money-order, telegraph, and Southern Express Co.'s offices; numerous orange groves; 3 miles from magnesia springs; good boating, hunting, and fishing.

J. M. Craig, Agent, F. S. R. R.
C. M. Haile, Agent, F. C. & P. R. R.
Commercial Hotel.—W. S. Moore, Proprietor. $2 per day, $20 to $40 per month.
Hawthorne House.—J. M. Berkstresser, Proprietor. $1.50 per day, $5 per week, $16 to $30 per month.

Hegman, Pasco Co., Florida.—P. O. name for **Abbot**, Florida.

Heidtville, Marion Co., Florida.—Five miles from Leroy.

J. W. Jordan will give information.

Hermitage, Gadsden Co., Florida.—Near Mt. Pleasant.

Hernando, Citrus Co., Florida.—Station on the S. S., O. & G. R. R., on Lake Tslapopka; population of the community, 200; good boating and fishing.

W. G. Crait will give information.
J. E. Westbrook.—Private board; $1 per day or $12 per month.

Herndon, Burke Co., Georgia.—On the main stem of the C. R. R. of Georgia.

Herndon Hotel.—J. B. Jones, Proprietor. Fifty yards from the station; accommodates 20; $1.50 per day, $15 per month.

Highland, Clay Co., Florida.—Station on the Southern Division of the F. C. & P. R. R.; population, 300; telegraph and Southern Express Co.'s offices.

H. C. Wimbleton, Agent, F. C. & P. R. R.
Palmetto House.—Hipple & Co., Proprietors. Accommodates 20; $1 per day and upward.

Highland Park, Volusia Co., Florida.—Station on the J., T. & K. W. Ry.; Glenwood, distant 2 miles, is nearest telegraph and Southern Express Co.'s offices.

D. B. Dibben will give information.

Hilliard, Nassau Co., Florida.—Station on the S., F. & W. Ry.; take S., F. & W. direct from Savannah; population of the community, 500; telegraph and Southern Express Co.'s office.

H. J. Davis will give information.
Stewart House.—G. T. Stewart, Proprietor. Accommodates 25; $2 per day, $10 per week, $25 per month. (Hotel temporarily closed.)

Hollister, Putnam Co., Florida.—Station on the F. S. Ry. Division of the J., T. & K. W. system; population of community about 200; Southern Express Co.'s office; nearest telegraph and money-order offices, Interlachen.

T. W. Ralph, Agent, Florida Southern R. R.
Mrs. J. Ralph.—Private board; 75 yards from the station; $1 per day, $6 per week, $15 per month.

SOUTHERN PRODUCTS TRANSPORTED PROMPTLY.

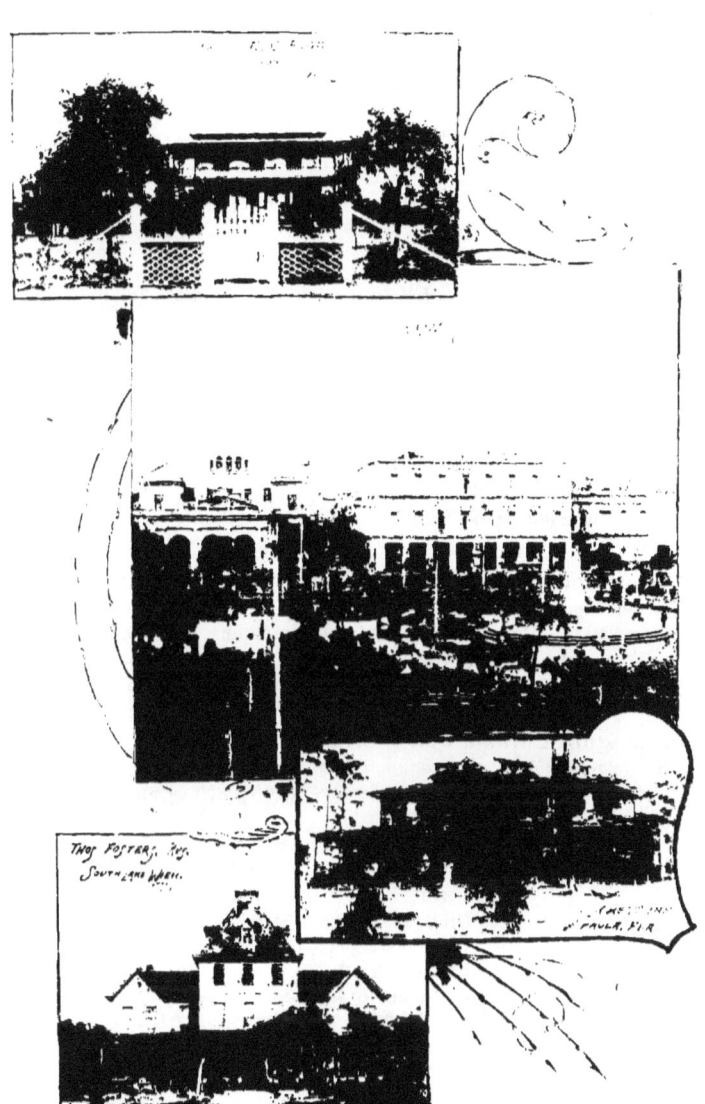

Holly Hill, Volusia Co., Florida.—On the west bank of the Halifax River, near Daytona, Florida; population of the community about 100.
  H. A. Carter will give information.

Holmes, Holmes Co., Florida.—Fifteen miles from Westville.

Homeland, Polk Co., Florida.—On the C. H. Division of the Florida Southern Ry.; telegraph and Southern Express Co.'s offices.
  T. W. Anderson, Agent, Florida Southern Ry.

Homosassa, Citrus Co., Florida.—On the Homosassa River; station on the S. S., O. & G. R. R.; population of the community about 150; telegraph and Southern Express Co.'s offices; hunting, boating, and fishing.
  John C. Jenkins will give information.
  Homosassa Inn.—A. E. Willard, Proprietor. Accommodates 50; $3 to $3.50 per day, $15 to $17.50 per week.

Horti, Brevard Co., Florida.—On the Banana River; nearest railroad station, Titusville; 2½ miles to ocean beach; reached by sail boat; good fishing and game in abundance.
  J. J. Fox.—Private board. Accommodates 20; $1.50 per day, $8 per week.

Hudson, Pasco Co., Florida.—On the Gulf of Mexico, 16 miles from Tarpon Springs, and 60 miles from Cedar Key; reached by boat from Clearwater Harbor; population of the community about 500; curiosity in way of a boiling spring.
  Moseley House.—M. L. Moseley, Proprietor. Two hundred yards from the station. Accommodates about 50; $1 per day, $5 per week, $16 per month.

Huntington, Putnam Co., Florida.—Station on the J., T. & K. W. Ry.; population of the community about 300; in the midst of high pine lands, with bearing orange groves; church, school, and amusement hall; express and telegraph office.
  "Qui-si-sana."—K. B. Huntington, Proprietor. Summer address, Stamford, Connecticut. Accommodates 20; $2 per day, $7 to $10 per week, $25 to $30 per month.
  K. B. Huntington will give information.

Hurtsboro, Russell Co., Alabama.—Station on the S. & W. Division of the C. R. R. of Georgia; population, 500; money-order, Southern Express Co.'s, and telegraph office.
  Davis House.—W. T. Davis, Proprietor. $1 per day and upward.
  Powell House.—S. S. Powell, Proprietor. $1 per day and upward.
  J. A. Rowland, Agent, C. R. R. of Georgia.

Hypoluxo, Dade Co., Florida.—South end of Lake Worth; nearest railroad station, Titusville; reached via Indian River Steamers.
  H. D. Pierce will give information.

Iamonia, Leon Co., Florida.—On Iamonia Lake, 17 miles from Thomasville, Georgia; population of the community about 200; good hunting; duck, geese, woodcock, snipe, and good fishing.
  D. A. Dickson will give information.
  C. P. Davis.—Private board. Accommodates 25; $2 per day, $10 per week, $40 per month.

Iddo, Taylor Co., Florida.—Fifteen miles from Madison, Florida.

TICKETS INCLUDE MEALS AND BERTH.

Indian River.—This is a most remarkable stream—a freak of nature—a stream of water 200 miles long, varying in width from a few yards to 8 miles, along the eastern coast of Florida, fed by inlets from the Atlantic, and all along the coast only a short distance from the ocean, at some points the ocean being only a few yards distant, while at others it is 3 to 5 miles. Well known to all Florida visitors, affording splendid aquatic sports and good hunting.

G. D. Ackerly, G. P. A., J., T. & K. W. system, Jacksonville, Florida; C. H. Bent, Superintendent, I. R. S. B. Co., Titusville, Florida; R. P. Paddison, Manager, East Coast Transportation Co., Titusville, will give information.

Indian Springs, Lake Co., Florida.—Three miles from Mt. Dora; population of the community about 100.

Walter Addison.—Private boarding; $1.50 per day, $18 per month.
W. R. Clark will give information.

Interlachen, Putnam Co., Florida.—On the Florida Southern Ry. Division of the J., T. & K. W. system; population of the community about 500; money-order, telegraph, and Southern Express Co.'s office; in the midst of bearing orange groves; 2 beautiful lakes; high, rolling land.

C. A. Brush, Agent, Florida Southern Ry.
Hotel Interlachen.—Interlachen Winter Resort Co., Proprietor; Charles R. Knapp, Manager. One block from the station; accommodates 75; $2 to $2.50 per day, $8 to $12 per week, $30 to $40 per month.
The Lagonda.—F. S. Roberts, Proprietor.
The Lake View.—L. A. Ross, Proprietor.
A. Chase (private board).—$6 to $10 per week.

Inverness, Bullock Co., Alabama.—Station on the Savannah & Western Division of the C. R. R. of Georgia; 9 miles from Union Springs; population of the community, 100; telegraph and Southern Express Co.'s office; in the midst of a good farming country.

W. R. Walker, Agent, C. R. R. of Georgia.
McKinnon House.—Mrs. S. McKinnon, Proprietor. Accommodates 10; $2 per day, special by the week.

Iola, Calhoun Co., Florida.—On the Apalachicola River; population of the community about 200; good hunting and fishing.

Day & Puckett will give information.
The Chipola.—W. E. Puckett, Proprietor. Accommodates 50; $2 per day, $10 per week, $20 per month.

Iona, Clay Co., Florida.—Six miles from Starke; population of the community about 100.

J. C. Blanchard will give information.
Mrs. J. Howe.—Private board; $1 per day, $5 per week, $15 to $18 per month.

Island Grove, Alachua Co., Florida.—Station on the Southern Division of the F. C. & P. R. R.; population of the community about 500; duck shooting, fishing, and boating; large bearing orange groves.

B. F. Carson, Agent, F. C. & P. R. R.
Island Grove House.—W. H. Cassels, Proprietor. $1 per day, $1.50 per week, $12.50 per month.
Meadford House.—M. D. Meadford, Proprietor. $1 per day, $1.50 per week, $12 per month.

ALWAYS TRAVEL VIA THE SAVANNAH LINE.

Island Lake, Orange Co., Florida.—On Orange Belt Ry.

Izagora, Alachua Co., Florida.—Landing on the Choctawhatchee River, 12 miles from Caryville.

Jacksonville, Duval Co., Florida.—Situated on the St. John's River, 24 miles from its mouth; population, 25,000; the metropolis of the State; headquarters for supplies; terminus of eight railways; the Union Passenger Station is the station at which passengers via **The Savannah Line** arrive on the Savannah, Florida & Western Ry., and from which trains of the Jacksonville, Tampa & Key West Ry. system, the Jacksonville, St. Augustine & Halifax River Ry., and steamers on the St. John's River leave; through Pullman cars into South Florida, from Savannah, pass through this station in Jacksonville. The Florida Central & Peninsula R. R. Passenger Station is near by.

Jacksonville is noted for its excellent, complete, and numerous hotels, among which are many equal in appointment and service to any in the world; has 4 daily papers, 2 morning and 2 evening; street-car lines extend throughout the city; gas; electric lights; water-works, supplied from artesian wells, flowing 5,000,000 gallons per day; churches of all denominations; 9 banks, with ample capital; fine opera-house. The health of Jacksonville is far above the average.

Florida Headquarters for The Savannah Line of steamers and the Central R. R. of Georgia are at No. 71 West Bay Street, where our patrons, friends, and the public generally are always welcome, and where information can be obtained, and state-rooms on steamers or berths in Pullman cars, to any point, can be secured.

W. H. Lucas, Florida Passenger Agent, will take pleasure in giving any information, either by mail or upon personal inquiry, or

B. R. Price, General Agent, will cheerfully attend to any matters relative to freight.

The St. James Hotel.—J. R. Campbell, Proprietor; C. O. Chamberlin, Superintendent. Facing St. James' Park; has telegraph and ticket office, where full information relative to Florida tours can be obtained, also through tickets to all points North, East, and West; livery connected; all the appointments of a first-class hotel; accommodates 500; $4 per day, $21 per week and upward. Proprietor's summer address, care Wilder & Co., 220 Devonshire Street, Boston.

Windsor Hotel.—Mrs. W. Van Hamm, Cincinnati, Ohio, owner; M. A. Fuller, Manager; on Hogan, Duval, and Adams Streets. $4 per day and upward, $21 per week; first class throughout.

Everett Hotel.—Melver & Baker, Proprietors; on Bay, Forsyth, and Julia Streets; telegraph and ticket office; livery connected; everything first class; accommodates 800; $3 per day and upward, $17.50 per week and upward.

The Travelers' Hotel.—Burton K. Burrs, Proprietor; corner Bay and Clay Streets; accommodates 100; $2 per day, $10 per week, $40 per month.

Carleton Hotel.—Corner Bay and Market Streets.

The Grand View Hotel.—G. W. Smith, Proprietor; Forsyth and Clay Streets; summer address, East View House, Bethlehem, N. H.; all the modern improvements; accommodates 80 to 100; $2 to $3 per day, $10 to $17.50 per week, $36 to $70 per month and upward.

The Tremont.—Dodge & Cullen, Proprietors; corner Forsyth and Newnan Streets.

The Duval.—S. H. Peck, Proprietor; corner Forsyth and Hogan Streets; accommodates 100; $2.50 to $3 per day.

St. John's House.—Mrs. Hudnell, Proprietor; 41 West Forsyth Street; accommodates 100; $2 to $2.50 per day, $8 to $12 per week, table board $6 to $7 per week.

New York House.—B. L. Hearn, Proprietor. Summer address, Atlanta, Georgia; accommodates 60; $1.50 per day, $7.50 per week, $25 per month.

The Savannah Line is prepared to

Acme Hotel.—H. A. Burt, Proprietor; 111 West Bay Street; accommodates 100; rooms 50 cents to $1 per day. $2.50 to $5 per week, without board.
Bettelini Hotel.—No. 16 East Bay Street; accommodates 150; rooms 25 cents per night and $1.25 to $2 per week.
Arlington Hotel.—Accommodates 75; $1.50 to $2 per day, $7 per week.
The Warner House.—Cole & Son, Proprietors. Corner Laura and Union Streets; accommodates 50; $2.50 per day, $10 to $14 per week.
The Reviere House.—Mrs. Oachus, Proprietor. Corner Ocean and Adams Streets; accommodates 35; $7 to $10 per week.
The Winter Home Boarding-House.—Mrs. Maxey, Proprietor. 92 East Forsyth Street; $1 per day, $6 per week.
The Bristol Hotel.—Mrs. Townsend, Proprietor. Corner Bay and Liberty Streets; accommodates 45; rooms $3 per week.
Ward House.—Mrs. Ward, Proprietor. Corner Julia and Forsyth Streets; accommodates 20; $2 per day, $10 to $14 per week.
The Oakland Grove House.—Corner Hogan and Ashby Streets; accommodates 15; $1.50 per day, $5 to $7 per week.
The Gary House.—Mrs. Gary, Proprietor. 91 West Forsyth Street; accommodates 6; board $4 per week, rooms $1.50 per week; room and board $5 per week.
The Willard.—Mrs. Reed, Proprietor. Accommodates 20; $2 per day, $7 per week.
Mrs. M. A. Gould.—Corner Hogan and Union Streets; accommodates 15; $1 per day, $6 per week.
Mrs. McGowan.—Corner Laura and Beaver Streets; accommodates 20; $2 per day, $10 per week.
Mr. J. S. Willis.—36 Julia Street; a room no later 7; $1 per day, $7 per week.
Mrs. Brown.—38 Julia Street; boarding-house; accommodates 12; $5 per week.
The Charleston.—Accommodates 20; furnished rooms; 50 cents to $1 per day, $2 to $5 per week.
The Thebeaut Building.—Charles Thebeaut, Proprietor. Corner Forsyth and Newnan Streets; accommodates 20; rooms $2 per week, $6.50 per month.
Mrs. Love.—90 West Adams Street; boarding-house; accommodates 20; $1 per day, $5 per week.
Continental Restaurant.—J. A. Walker, Proprietor. 97 West Bay Street; accommodates 50; meals 50 cents; rooms 50 cents, 75 cents, and $1.
Marion's Restaurant.—33 East Bay Street; accommodates 32; single meals 30 cents board by the week $5.
City Dining Hall.—Meals 40 cents; $5 per week; accommodates 40.
La Belle Restaurant.—Accommodates 20; meals 40 cents, board by the week $6.25.
Chinese Restaurant.—Way Lee, Proprietor. 64 West Bay Street; accommodates 40; meals 30 cents, board by the week $4.
Acme Hotel Restaurant.—J. H. Burt, Proprietor. Accommodates 255; single meal 30 cents, board by the week $5.
West End Restaurant.—D. C. Andress, Proprietor. Accommodates 25; single meal 30 cents, $5 per week.
The Johnson House.—Mrs. Caburn, Proprietor. Accommodates 35; $6 to $8 per week.

Jasper, Hamilton Co., Florida.—Station on the S., F. & W., and also on the G. S. & F.; population, 700; money-order, telegraph, and Southern Express Co.'s office; Devil's Cave; Sinks of Allapaha River; pear groves.

Hateley House.—Mrs. Z. Hateley, Proprietor. Two hundred yards from the station $2 per day, $10 per week, $30 per month.
Hamilton House.—Mrs. M. G. Small, Proprietor. $1 to $2 per day, $12 to $20 per month.

Jekyl Island (P. O. at **Brunswick, Ga.**), **Glynn Co., Georgia.**—Off the coast of Georgia, 7 miles from Brunswick; this island is the property of a private club.

S. F. Finney, Secretary, or E. G. Grob, Superintendent, may be addressed for information.

handle freight more promptly than others.

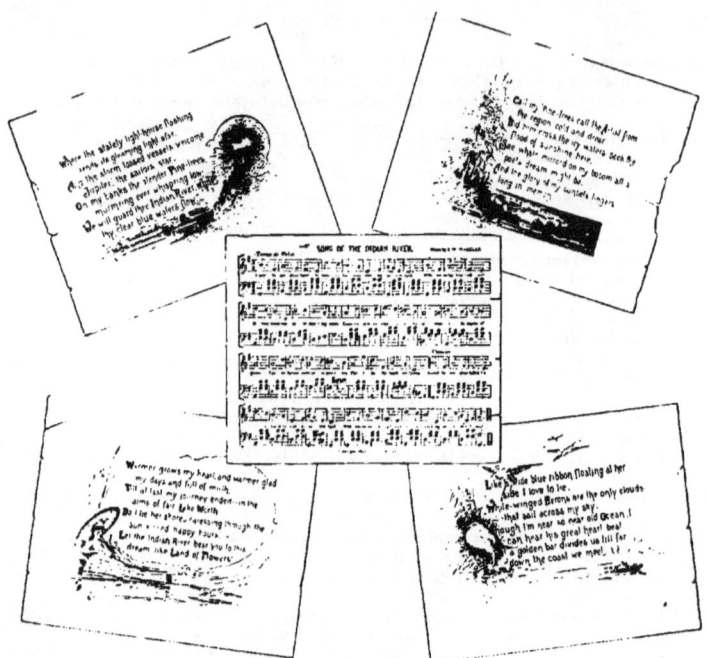

THE SONG OF INDIAN RIVER.

REPRODUCED FROM
PHOTOGRAPH TAKEN AT ST. LUCIE, ON INDIAN RIVER
DECEMBER 5, 1890.

Jennings, Hamilton Co., Florida.—Station on the G. S. & F. R. R.; population of the community about 300.

Jensen, Brevard Co., Florida.—On the Indian River, 2½ miles from Eden; a community of 35 families; nearest railroad station, Titusville.
John Sorensen will give information.

Jessamine, Pasco Co., Florida.—One and one-half miles from Blanton, and 5 miles from San Antonio.
W. N. Pike will give information.

Jewell, Dade Co., Florida.—Near Lake Worth.

Johnson, Putnam Co., Florida.—Station on the F. S. Ry. Div. of the J., T. & K. W. system.
D. W. Johnson, Agent, Florida Southern Ry., will give information.

Jonesboro, Clayton Co., Georgia.—Station on the main stem of the C. R. R. of Ga.; population, 1000; money-order, telegraph, and Southern Express Co.'s office.
W. F. Heidt, Agent, C. R. R. of Ga.
Hutchison House.—Mrs. Hutchison, Proprietor.
Jones Hotel.—Mrs. Georgia Jones, Proprietor. $2 per day.

Jonesville, Alachua Co., Florida.—Nine miles from Archer.

Judson, Levy Co., Florida.—Fifteen miles from Bronson.

Juliette (P. O. name Blue Spring), Marion Co., Florida.—Station on the S. S., O. & G. R. R.; population of the community, 150; 20 miles from Ocala, is nearest money-order, telegraph, and Southern Express Co.'s office; heart of the phosphate region, and head of Blue Springs.

Juno, Dade Co., Florida.—At the head of Lake Worth, and southern terminus of the Jupiter & Lake Worth R. R.; telephone, connecting with telegraph at Jupiter.
Juno Hotel.—Washington Jenkins, Proprietor.
Lake View.—E. Peterson, Proprietor. $1.50 per day, $5 per week, $20 per month and upward.
A. M. Field, Agent, J., L. & W. R. R.

Jupiter, Dade Co., Florida.—At the mouth of the Indian River, on Jupiter Inlet; northern terminus of the Jupiter & Lake Worth R. R.; reached via Indian River; population of the community about 50; telegraph office; good fishing and hunting, and excellent winter climate, for all of which it is celebrated the world over.
J. S. Matheson, Agent, I. R. S. B. Co.
Vaill's Floating Hotel.—E. E. Vaill, Proprietor. Accommodates 60; $3 per day, $17.50 per week.
Carlin House.—J. H. Carlin, Proprietor. Accommodates 20; $2.50 per day, $12 per week, $40 per month and upward.

Kanapaha, Alachua Co., Florida.—Station on the Cedar Key Division of the F. C. & P. R. R.; good hunting and fishing; quail, snipe, ducks, squirrels.
A. R. Elmore, Agent, F. C. & P. R. R.
A. R. Elmore.—Private board; $1.50 per day, $6 per week, $20 per month.

THE FASTEST PASSENGER STEAMSHIPS

Kathleen, Polk Co., Florida.—Station on the Pemberton Ferry Branch of the South Florida R. R.; population about 400; 6 miles from Lakeland; Southern Express Co.'s office; nearest money-order and telegraph office at Lakeland.

J. B. Turner will give information.
Private boarding-houses by H. A. Prim and J. L. Lanier; $1 per day, $5 per week and upward.

Kelly, Osceola Co., Florida.—Station on the St. Cloud Sugar Belt Ry.; population of the community about 100; nearest post-office and station, St. Cloud, 2 miles distant.

John Kelly, President, Florida Rice Manufacturing Co., will give full information.

Kendrick, Marion Co., Florida.—Station on the F. S. Division of the J., T. & K. W. system; 5 miles from Ocala.

C. J. Grace will give information.
C. J. Grace.—Private board; $4 per week and upward.

Keuka (or Keuka Lake), Putnam Co., Florida.—Station on the Florida Southern Ry. Division of the J., T. & K. W. system; population of the community, 200; telegraph and Southern Express Co.'s office; beautiful lakes and orange groves; 1 mile to Keuka Springs; 6 miles to Ocklawaha River.

Edward Rumley will give information.
H. B. Locke, Agent, Florida Southern Ry.
Lake View Hotel.—J. M. Leedy, Proprietor. $1 per day, $5 per week, $20 per month.
Mrs. Sarah Andrews.—Private board at reasonable rates.

Keysville, Hillsboro Co., Florida.—Nearest railroad station, Plant City, 11 miles.

M. M. Blue will give information.
The Riverside.—Mrs. D. M. Blue, Proprietor. By hack from the railroad station; reasonable rates.

Key West, Monroe Co., Florida.—Most southerly city in the United States, on an island in the Gulf of Mexico; Plant Line Steamers, en route to and from Havana or Port Tampa, Florida, always remain at Key West for 3 or 4 hours; population, 20,000; known the world over as a great cigar-manufacturing city; many attractions.

R. W. Southwick, Agent, Plant S. S. Line, will give information.
New Russell House.—C. T. Merrill, Proprietor. One-quarter mile from the steamer landing by phaeton. Accommodates 100; $3.50 per day and upward.
The Duval House.—Mrs. J. Bolio, Proprietor. Accommodates 30; $2.50 to $3 per day, $17 per week.
The Victoria Hotel.—J. A. Escobar, Proprietor (American and European plans). Accommodates 50; $2.50 to $3 per day, $15 per week.

Killarney, Orange Co., Florida.—On the Orange Belt Ry., and on the T. & G. R. R.; hunting and fishing; two lakes near by.

B. M. Burdett will give information.

King's Ferry, Nassau Co., Florida.—On the St. Mary's River, 9 miles from Hilliard.

Kinsley, Clay Co., Florida.—Six miles from Lawtey; population of the community about 100.

Preddy House.—Richard Preddy, Proprietor. $1 per day, $20 per month.

FLYING THE AMERICAN FLAG.

Kissimmee, Osceola Co., Florida.—Junction of the South Florida R. R. and the St. Cloud Sugar Belt R. R.; also a station on the Florida Midland; population, 1500; on the shores of Lake Tohoptkelika; in the midst of large sugar and rice plantations; fine fishing, good shooting, boating, and driving.

E. P. Tabeau, Agent, South Florida R. R.
J. W. Aderhold will give information.
Tropical Hotel.—George F. Goode, Proprietor. Near the station. Accommodates 200 $3 per day, $10 to $17 per week.
City Hotel.—E. T. Smith, Proprietor. Accommodates 75; $2 per day, $7 per week.
South Florida House.—Mrs. Rushton, Proprietor. Accommodates 75; $1.50 per day, $6 per week, $20 per month.
Broadway House.—J. P. Peeler, Proprietor. Accommodates 40; $2 per day, $7 per week.
Kissimmee House.—J. W. Seymour, Proprietor. Accommodates 50; $1.50 per day, $6 per week.

La Crosse, Schley Co., Georgia.—Station on the S. & W. Division of the C. R. R. of Ga.; population of the community about 300.

Lady Lake, Lake Co., Florida.—Eight miles from Leesburg; population of the community, 300.

J. T. Stapleton, Agent, Florida Southern Ry.
Lake House.—Mrs. S. B. Sligh. Accommodates 25; $1.50 per day, $7 per week, $25 per month.

Lafayette, Chambers Co., Alabama.—On the S. & W. Division of the C. R. R. of Ga.; population, 1500; money-order, telegraph, and Southern Express Co.'s office.

R. L. Baugh, Agent, C. R. R. of Ga.
McKenzie House.—Mrs. J. McKensie, Proprietor. Accommodates 40; 200 yards from the station; $2 per day, $7 per week, $20 per month.
Central Hotel.—Mrs. S. E. McLemore, Proprietor. Two hundred yards from the station $2 per day, $7 per week, $20 per month.

Lake Ashby, Volusia Co., Florida.—On Lake Ashby, a clear-water lake, 3 miles long and 2 miles wide; 3 miles from Lake Ashby station; 8 miles from Osteen.

Lake Charm, Orange Co., Florida.—Terminus of the S. & I. R. Division of the South Florida R. R.; three-quarter mile from Oviedo; in the midst of a good orange country; near the shores of Lake Jesup.

O. H. Brewster will give information.
Lake Charm Hotel.—Crane & Pfiefer, Managers. Accommodates 50; $2 per day; special rates by the week or month.

Lake City, Columbia Co., Florida.—On the S., F. & W. Ry., also on F. C. & P. R. R.; population, 2500; money-order, telegraph, and Southern Express Co.'s office; seat of the U. S. Experiment Station, Florida State Agricultural College, Peabody High-School, and Lake City Institute.

S. Boteler Thompson will give information.
Central Hotel.—T. M. Brantley, Manager. Accommodates 45; near the station; $2 per day, $10 per week, $30 per month.
he Inn.—Jno. H. Gee, Proprietor. Accommodates 20; near the station; $2 per day, $10 per week, $25 per month.

The Savannah Line Steamers are the Finest.

Lake Como (or Como), Putnam Co., Florida.—Station on the J., T. & K. W. R. R.; 300 people in the community; Southern Express Co.'s office; good fishing and sailing on Lake Como.

Avenue House.—C. T. Potter. Accommodates 40; $1.50 per day, $7 to $9 per week, $25 to $30 per month; several private boarding-houses at $1 per day.
Address W. E. Palmer, Agent, J., T. & K. W. Ry., or C. T. Potter, for information.

Lake Helen, Volusia Co., Florida.—On Lake Helen; station on the Atlantic & Western R. R.; in the midst of clear spring-water lakes; orange groves and high pine lands; population of the community, 400.

Granville House.—Accommodates 40; 160 rods from the station by hack; $2.50 per day, $10 per week and upwards.
Harlan Hotel.—H. A. De Land, Owner. Accommodates 100; one-half mile from the station by hack; $2 per day and upward; special rates by the week or month.

Lake Kerr, Marion Co., Florida.—Eight miles west of the St. John's River, 8 miles from Norwalk Landing; population of the community about 50.

R. K. Willmott will give information.
Lake Kerr House.—O. Hammond, Proprietor. Hack will meet steamer. Accommodates 50; $1 per day, $5 per week.

Lakeland, Polk Co., Florida.—Junction of the main line of the South Florida R. R. and the Pemberton Ferry Branch; population, 700; money-order, telegraph, and Southern Express Co.'s office; numerous lakes, affording excellent fishing, boating, and hunting; good roads for driving; one of the highest points in South Florida.

C. H. Keller, Agent, South Florida R. R.
Tremont House.—J. H. A. Bruce, Manager. One hundred yards from the station. $2.50 to $3 per day, $10 to $17.50 per week, $35 to $50 per month.
Commercial Hotel.—John Jackson, Proprietor. $2 per day; special rates by the week or month.
Florida House.—L. M. Ballard, Proprietor. $1.50 per day, special rates by the week or month.

Lake Mary, Orange Co., Florida.—Station on the South Florida R. R.; 5 miles south of Sanford.

W. N. Webster will give information.

UNEQUALED FACILITIES.

Lakeview, Clay Co., Florida.—Eight miles from Starke; population of the community about 100; fine bathing, boating, and fishing on Lake Kinsley, one-half mile distant.
E. E. Richmond will give information.

Lakeville, Orange Co., Florida.—On the Orange Belt Ry.; population, 150; rolling pine lands; in the midst of clear-water lakes; 60-acre bearing orange grove near by.
George H. Rines, Agent, Orange Belt Ry., will give information.

Lake Worth, Dade Co., Florida.—On Lake Worth; population of the community about 300; reached by way of the Indian River and J. & L. W. R. R.; fine hunting and fishing; sea bathing.
Hotel Lake Worth.– H. P. Dye, Proprietor. Thirty yards from the landing; will accommodate 80; $3 to $4 per day, $15 to $25 per week.

Lamont, Jefferson Co., Florida.—Ten miles from Aucilla.
S. B. Smith will give information.
R. R. Ledbetter.–Private board. Accommodates 25; $2 per day, $5 to $10 per week.

Lane Park, Lake Co., Florida.—Station on the F. S. Ry. Division of the J., T. & K. W. system; population of the community about 400; telegraph and Southern Express Co.'s office.

Lanier, Lake Co., Florida.—Station on the Florida Southern Ry., 5 miles from Leesburg; beautiful lakes; large orange groves.
T. C. Lanier will give information.
The Lake View.—Mrs. Gray, Manager. Accommodates about 100; reasonable rates.

Largo, Hillsboro Co., Florida.—Station on the Orange Belt Ry.; population of the community about 400; 3 miles from Clearwater Harbor, 2 miles from the Gulf; situated on Lake Largo; fine fishing, boating, and bathing.
Oak Grove House.—Wm. J. Taylor, Proprietor. Within 20 yards of the station; accommodates 10; $1 per day, $4 per week, $15 per month and upward.
Dewar House.—A. Dewar, Proprietor. Accommodates about 15; $1 per day, $5 per week, $15 per month and upward.
Wm. J. Taylor will give information.

Lawtey, Bradford Co., Florida.—Station on the Southern Division F. C. & P. R. R., in the midst of the strawberry section of the State; population of the community, 500; telegraph and Southern Express Co.'s office.
V. J. Shipman, Agent, F. C. & P. R. R.
Burrin House.—T. J. Burrin, Proprietor. Accommodates about 40; $2 per day, $6 to $10 per week and upward.

Leary, Calhoun Co., Georgia.—On the South-western Division of the C. R. R. of Ga.; telegraph and Southern Express Co.'s office; artesian water; fine fishing; plenty of both large and small game.
J. E. Mercer, Agent, C. R. R. of Ga.
Griffen House.—T. P. Griffen, Proprietor. One hundred yards from the station; accommodates 40; $2 per day, $10 per week, $25 per month.

Lebanon, Levy Co., Florida.—Near Dunnellon.
C. C. Gaines will give information.

THE SAVANNAH LINE IS PREPARED TO

Lee, Madison Co., Florida.—Station on the F. C. & P. R. R., near Madison.

Leesburg, Lake Co., Florida.—Station on the Florida Southern Ry. Division of the J., T. & K. W. system, and on the Southern Division of the F. C. & P. R. R.; located between lakes Griffin and Harris, both navigable lakes, the shores of which are dotted with orange-bearing groves; population, 1500; money-order, telegraph, and Southern Express Co.'s offices; there is located here the State Methodist College, one of the finest opera-houses in the State; and 4 churches.

<small>B. F. Watts, Agent, Florida Southern Ry., or G. R. Haile, Agent, F. C. & P. R. R., will give information.
Lake View Hotel (winter hotel).—Davis Tillson, Owner, Rockland, Me.; William Gray, Manager. Accommodates 75 to 100; $3 per day, special by the week or month.
Union Hotel.—E. A. Protois, Proprietor. $3 per day, $15 per week, special by the month; accommodates 40.
Central Hotel.—J. D. Pendleton, Proprietor. Accommodates 50 to 60; $1.50 to $2 per day, $6 to $7 per week, special rates by the month.
Kentucky House.—S. E. Fuller, Proprietor. Accommodates 30; $1.50 per day, $7 per week, $20 to $25 per month.
Numerous private boarding-houses at reasonable rates.</small>

Lenard, Pasco Co., Florida.—Station on the Orange Belt Ry.; population of the community, 200; Southern Express Co.'s and telegraph office. Lake fishing; good drives.

<small>C. F. Kuster, Agent, Orange Belt Ry.
W. S. Kuster.—Private board.</small>

Leroy, Marion Co., Florida.—Station on the S. S., O. & G. R. R., 13 miles from Ocala; good farming section, and thrifty.

<small>The Matanzas.—Accommodates 40; $2 per day, $7.50 per week, $25 per month.
The Leroy.—Accommodates 30; $1.50 per day, $6 per week, $20 per month.</small>

Limona, Hillsboro Co., Florida.—Station on the Tampa Division of the F. C. & P. R. R.; telegraph and Southern Express Co.'s office; population of the community, 125; high, rolling country; in the midst of numerous lakes.

<small>E. E. Pratt, Agent, F. C. & P. R. R.</small>

Live Oak, Suwanee Co., Florida.—Station on the S., F. & W., direct from Savannah, also on the Western Division of the F. C. & P. R. R.; population of the community, 3000; money-order, telegraph, and Southern Express Co.'s office; high, healthy, and shady; fine churches, high-school; no bar-rooms.

<small>C. H. McGehee, Agent, F. C. & P. R. R., and J. C. Little, Agent, S. F. & W. Ry., will give information.
Ethel House.—B. B. Blackwell, Proprietor. $1 to $2 per day, $5 to $12 per week, $15 to $40 per month.
Live Oak House.—J. W. Kennedy, Proprietor. $1 to $2 per day, $5 to $12 per week, $15 to $40 per month.</small>

Liverpool, De Soto Co., Florida.—On the Charlotte Harbor Division of the Florida Southern Ry.

HANDLE FREIGHT MORE PROMPTLY THAN OTHERS.

Lloyd, Jefferson Co., Florida.—Station on the Western Division of the F. C. & P. R. R.; population of the community about 500; telegraph and Southern Express Co.'s office.

> E. Wickham, Agent, F. C. & P. R. R.
> **Whitfield House.**—W. A. Snyder, Manager. Accommodates 25; near the station; $2 per day, $5 to $6 per week.

Lochbie, Marion Co., Florida.—On the F. S. Ry. Division of the J., T. & K. W. system; population of the community, 700; telegraph and Southern Express Co.'s office.

Lochloosa, Alachua Co., Florida.—Station on the Southern Division of the F. C. & P. R. R.; population of the community about 300; Southern Express Co.'s office; Hawthorne, 6 miles distant, is nearest money-order and telegraph office; fine hunting and fishing; boating on the lake.

> **Lochloosa House.**—A. Roundtree, Proprietor. $1.50 per day, $6 per week, $20 per month.
> A. K. Wade, Agent, F. C. & P. R. R.

Longwood, Orange Co., Florida.—Junction of the South Florida R. R. and the Florida Midland Ry.; population of the community, 1500; fine hammock drives; excellent fishing and shooting.

> E. W. Henck will give information.
> G. L. Seibert, Agent, South Florida R. R. and Florida Midland Ry.
> **Hotel Waltham.**—Carl Cushing, Proprietor. Accommodates 75; near the station; $2.50 per day, special arrangements by the week or month.

Lynne, Marion Co., Florida.—Seven miles from Grahamville; landing on the Ocklawaha River.

> M. L. Series will give information.

Macon, Bibb Co., Georgia.—One of the principal stations on the C. R. R. of Ga.; population, 23,000; 10 railroads centre here; Young Men's College; Mercer University; Young Ladies' Wesleyan College; State Fair; Home of Southern Cadets, a celebrated military company; Union Depot.

> D. H. Bythewood, Passenger Agent, R. & D. and Central R. R., will give information.
> **Hotel Lanier.**—J. D. Crawford, Proprietor. Accommodates 300; $3 to $4 per day, $17 to $21 per week.
> **Brown House.**—J. D. Sperry, Proprietor. Accommodates 250; $3 to $4 per day, $17 to $21 per week.

Magnolia Springs, Clay Co., Florida.—On the St. John's River, and also a station on the J., T. & K. W. R. R.; winter resort; mineral spring; very fine hammock growth; beautifully located; fishing, hunting; hotel fully equipped with pleasure boats, launches, &c., affording delightful trip on St. John's River and up beautiful creeks.

> **Magnolia Springs Hotel and Cottages.**—J. S. Fay, Boston, Mass., Owner; A. C. Coleman, Manager. Summer address, Everett House, New York. First class in every respect; accommodates 250; $3 per day, $21 per week and upward; reached from the station by tram car.

SOUTHERN PRODUCTS TRANSPORTED PROMPTLY.

Maitland, Orange Co., Florida.—Station on the South Florida R. R.; population of community, 600; money order, telegraph, and Southern Express Co.'s office; beautiful section; numerous lakes and bearing orange groves.

J. J. Heard, Agent, South Florida R. R.
Park House.—Accommodates 50; $2 to $3 per day and special rates by the week.
Maitland House.—Private board at reasonable rates.
Stith House.—Private board at reasonable rates.

Malabar, Brevard Co., Florida.—On the Indian River; population of the community about 100.

Manatee, Manatee Co., Florida.—On the Manatee River; population of the community 400; money-order office, telegraph, and Southern Express Co.'s office at Port Tampa; fishing, bathing, and hunting; great vegetable and orange section.

J. W. Jackson will give information.

Mango, Hillsboro Co., Florida.—Station on the South Florida R. R.; population of the community, 100.

Mannville, Putnam Co., Florida.—Station on the F. S. Ry. Division of the J., T. & K. W. system; 1½ miles from Interlachen; population of the community, 150; beautiful lakes; boating, fishing, and hunting; about 500 acres in young orange groves in the vicinity.

T. W. Abrahams will give information.
W. H. Mann.—Private board. Accommodates 30; $1 to $2 per day, $5 to $8 per week.

Marco, Lee Co., Florida.—On the gulf coast; population of the community about 300; nearest railroad station, Punta Gorda, reached from there by sail boat.

Mrs. Julia Crawford.—Private board. Accommodates 15; $1 to $2 per day, $3.50 to $5 per week, special by the month.
W. D. Colbir will give information.

Markham, Orange Co., Florida.—On the S. & L. E. Division of the J., T. & K. W. R. R., 3 miles from Paola.

Martel, Marion Co., Florida.—Station on the S. S., O. & G. R. R.; population of the community, 200; 7½ miles from Ocala.

W. Long will give information.

Mascotte, Lake Co., Florida.—Station on the Orange Belt Ry.; population of the community about 500.

J. K. Foster will give information.

Matanzas, St. John's Co., Florida.—Ten miles from Windermere; population of the community 150; 18 miles from St. Augustine.

J. L. Kennedy will give information.

Maxville, Washington Co., Florida.—(Bease Creek Ferry); located on Bease Creek; nearest railroad station, Chipley, 34 miles; fine mineral well located here, possessing many health-giving properties.
  The Maxville.—J. W. McAllister, Proprietor. Accommodates 40; by hack from Chipley; $1 per day, $6 per week, $25 per month.
  J. W. McAllister will give information.

Mayo, Orange Co., Florida.—(See Woodbridge.)

Mayo (or Mazo), Lafayette Co., Florida.—Landing on the Suwanee River, 18 miles from New Branford; hunting and fishing.
  W. T. Dees will give information.

Mayport, Duval Co., Florida.—On J. M. & P. R. R., near the mouth of the St. John's River; population about 500; fine fishing, sailing, and bathing; driving on the hard beach; good hunting; deer, turkey, quail, and other game.
  Burrows House.—L. S. Burrows, Proprietor. Accommodates 30; $2 per day, $8 to $10 per week, $25 to $35 per month.
  L. S. Burrows will give information.

McAlpin, Suwanee Co., Florida.—On the S., F. & W. R. R.; population of the community, 200; 12 miles from Live Oak.
  J. N. Altman will give information.

McClenny, Baker Co., Florida.—Station on the Western Division of the F. C. & P. R. R.
  George E. Abbott.—Private board, also Mrs. E. Barber; $1.50 per day, $5 per week, $18 per month and upward.

McIntosh, Marion Co., Florida.—Station on the F. S. Ry. Division of the J., T. & K. W. R. R.; population of the community about 100; Southern Express Co.'s office; nearest telegraph office, Boardman.
  M. T. Walker, Agent, Florida Southern Ry., or
  S. H. Gaitskill will give information.

McMeekin, Putnam Co., Florida.—Station on the F. S. Ry. Division of the J., T. & K. W. system; population of the community about 600; money-order, telegraph, and Southern Express Co.'s office.
  J. McMeekin, Agent, Florida Southern Ry.

McRae, Clay Co., Florida.—Four miles from Spring Lake; 18 miles from Starke.
  Lyman Hall will give information.

Melbourne, Brevard Co., Florida.—On the Indian River; population, 250; money-order and telegraph offices; fresh and salt water fishing; only three-quarter mile to the Atlantic Ocean for surf bathing; good hunting, quail and deer; pine-apple and orange groves; 3 churches; no saloons.
  S. F. Gibbs will give information.
  Carleton.—S. N. Carter, Proprietor. Near the landing; accommodates 40; $3 per day, special by the week or month.
  Riverside.—R. W. Goode, Proprietor. Near the landing; accommodates 25; $2 per day, special by the week or month.

Melrose, Alachua Co., Florida.—Station on the Western Ry. of Florida, and Santa Fé Canal Co., on Santa Fé Lake, which is 10 miles long, fed by springs; population of the community, 1000; money-order, telegraph, and Southern Express Co.'s office; a community of regular winter visitors.

<small>The Santa Fé.—I. F. Graham, Proprietor. Accommodates 100; $2 per day, $8 to $15 per week and upward.
Bay View.—Mrs. M. L. Lambdin, Proprietor.
M. L. Lambdin will give information.</small>

Merritt, Brevard Co., Florida.—On the Indian River, opposite Rockledge; hunting, fishing, boating, and bathing; artesian and spring water.

<small>P. J. Nevens will give information.
The River View.—P. J. Nevens, Proprietor. Summer address, 209 Duane Street, New York. Accommodates 50; $3 per day, $15 per week, $50 to $60 per month.</small>

Miakka, Manatee Co., Florida.—On the Miakka River, 20 miles from Manatee; population of the community, 150; boating, hunting, and fishing; large and small game.

<small>A. M. Wilson will give information.</small>

Miami, Dade Co., Florida.—On Biscayne Bay.

Micanopy, Alachua Co., Florida.—Station on the Florida Southern Ry. Division of the J., T. & K. W. system; population, 700; money-order, telegraph, and Southern Express Co.'s offices; numerous lakes; splendid fishing and hunting; good orange and vegetable section.

<small>C. E. Owens will give information.
Tuscawilla Hotel.—L. H. Johnson, Proprietor. Accommodates 50; $2 per day, $7 per week, $20 per month.</small>

Micco, Brevard Co., Florida.—Landing on the west bank of the Indian River, which is 2½ miles wide at this point; about 1000 yards across to the Atlantic Ocean.

<small>V. H. Harris will give information.
Bay View Cottage.—P. Koller, Proprietor. Three-quarter mile from the landing, by foot or in small boat; $7 per week.
Oak Lodge.—C. F. Latham, Proprietor. Three miles from the landing, in sail boat; $7 per week.
V. H. Harris.—(Private and transient board.) $2 per day, special by the week or month.</small>

Midland, Polk Co., Florida.—Ten miles from Fort Meade.

<small>J. C. Burleigh will give information.</small>

Midway, Gadsden Co., Florida.—Station on the Western Division of the F. C. & P. R. R.; population of the community, 500; Southern Express Co.'s office; Quincy is the nearest telegraph and money-order office.

<small>F. R. Centey, Agent, F. C. & P. R. R.
Arnold House.—Mrs. Henrietta Arnold, Proprietor. $1 per day, $5 per week, $18 per month.</small>

THE SAVANNAH LINE STEAMERS ARE THE FINEST.

Millen, Screven Co., Georgia.—On the main stem of the C. R. R. of Georgia; population, 1500; money-order, telegraph, and Southern Express Co.'s office.
C. W. Fox, Agent, C. R. R. of Georgia.
Millen Hotel.—Isadore Wilson, Manager. $2 per day, $10 per week, $20 to $35 per month.

Minneola, Lake Co., Florida.—Station on the Orange Belt and the Tavares & Gulf Rys.; population, 250; fine fishing and hunting; small game, such as quail, pigeons, and squirrels; in the midst of the vegetable-growing country and what is known as the Apopka Mountains.
Lake View House.—Mrs. E. Straker, Proprietor. Twenty rods from the station; accommodates 25; $1 per day, $5 to $7 per week, $18 to $20 per month.
Wm. G. Hanson will give information.

Mobile, Mobile Co., Alabama.—On Mobile Bay, on the line of the L. & N. R. R.; population, 40,000; reached via Savannah direct, or can be visited from Florida very conveniently, via Plant S. S. Line, from Port Tampa, or via rail lines from Jacksonville; pretty city; equable climate; beautiful shell road along the bay.
The Commercial Club will give information.
Accommodations can readily be secured at rates of $1 per day and upward. The following are some of the principal hotels and boarding-places:
Battle House.
Hotel Royal.
Hotel La Tourette.
Point Clear Hotel.—On the bay.
Spring Hill Hotel.—In the suburbs.
Mrs. Voorhees.—Church Street.
Mrs. Snow.—St. Emmanuel Street.
Mrs. Crawford.—Government Street.
Mrs. Douglas.—St. Joseph Street.
All easy of access by carriage, street car, or omnibus.

Mohawk (P. O. at Minneola, 1½ miles), Lake Co., Florida.—Finely located; beautiful scenery.
W. G. Hanson will give information.
Mohawk House.—A. Fillmore, Proprietor. Accommodates 10; $1 per day, $5 per week, $20 per month.

Montague, Marion Co., Florida.—On the F. S. Ry. Div. of the J., T. & K. W. system, 3½ miles from Ocala; a pleasant locality in the phosphate region; good orange country.
The Rose Hill.—Miss E. Wagoner, Proprietor. Accommodates 10; $1 per day, $5 per week, $20 per month.
T. W. Moore will give information.

Montclair, Lake Co., Florida.—On the Southern Division of the F. C. & P. R. R., 2½ miles from Leesburg; population of the community, 400.
W. T. Jamieson, Agent, F. C. & P. R. R.

Montezuma, Macon Co., Georgia.—Station on the South-western Division of the C. R. R. of Ga.; population, 1000; money-order, telegraph, and Southern Express Co.'s office; has 9 artesian wells; freestone, sulphur, and chalybeate waters.
C. A. Hamilton, Agent, C. R. R. of Ga.
Minor House.—P. C. Affleck, Proprietor. Accommodates 15; $2 per day, $10 per week, $30 per month.
Artesian Hotel.—McD. Felder, Proprietor. $2 per day, $.0 per week.

TICKETS INCLUDE MEALS AND BERTH.

Montgomery, Montgomery Co., Alabama.—Capital of the State, on the Alabama River, one of the northern termini of the C. R. R. of Ga.; this city and Atlanta are the gateways to Florida from the West and North-west; population, 30,000.
Exchange Hotel.—D. P. West, Proprietor. Accommodates 400; $2.50 to $3 per day, $17.50 per week, special by the month.
The Windsor.—D. P. West, Proprietor. Accommodates 250; $2.50 to $3 per day, $17.50 per week, special by the month.
Merchants' Hotel.—T. H. Mabson, Proprietor. Accommodates 100; $2 to $2.50 per day, $10 to $15 per week, $30 to $45 per month.
Mrs. James Jackson, No. 19 Madison Avenue.—Private board. $2 per day, $10 per week, $30 per month.

Monticello, Jefferson Co., Florida.—Station on the Western Division of the F. C. & P. R. R,; terminus of Monticello Branch of the S., F. & W. Ry.; reached direct from Savannah via S., F. & W. Ry.; population, 1800; money-order, telegraph, and Southern Express Co.'s offices; in the midst of fine, rolling farming country; beautiful large live oaks, very numerous and attractive.
B. W. Partridge or T. J. Wright will give information.
Partridge House.—B. W. Partridge, Proprietor. Accommodates 20; $2 per day, $10 to $12 per week.
Madden House.—M. C. Oakley, Proprietor. Accommodates 40; $2 per day, $10 to $12 per week.

Mt. Dora, Lake Co., Florida.—On the S. & L. E. Division of the J., T. & K. W. R. R.; money-order, telegraph, and Southern Express Co.'s office; population of the community about 500; in the midst of a beautiful orange and lake region; South Florida Chautauqua meets here during March and April.
A. F. Atterbery, Agent, J., T. & K. W. Ry.
Bruce House.—B. M. Bruce, Proprietor. Accommodates 40; $1.50 to $2 per day, $8 to $10 per week, $20 to $30 per month.
Lake House.—J. M. Alexander, Proprietor. Accommodates 20; $1.50 to $2 per day, $6 to $10 per week, $20 to $30 per month.
Several private boarding-houses at reasonable rates.

Mt. Pleasant, Gadsden Co., Florida.—On the Western Division of the F. C. & P. R. R.; population of the community about 100; 8 miles from Quincy; pine woods, rolling land; Glen Julia Springs one-quarter mile distant.
Wm. S. Lee, Agent, F. C. & P. R. R.
E. F. Sheppard and D. A. Strain.—Private boarding-houses; $1 per day, special by the week or month.

Mt. Tabor, Columbia Co., Florida.—Ten miles south of Lake City; population, 100.
Address M. A. English for information.

Myers (or Fort Myers), Lee Co., Florida.—Landing on the Caloosahachee River; reached by steamer from Punta Gorda; population, 900; money-order, telegraph, and Southern Express Co.'s office; tropical fruits and growth; fishing for tarpon and small fish; hunting quail, deer, turkey; sailing and boating.
Walter F. Mickle will give information.
Hendry House.—L. A. Hendry, Proprietor. Accommodates 50; 2 blocks from the landing; $2 per day, $10 per week, $30 per month and upward.

ALWAYS TRAVEL VIA THE SAVANNAH LINE.

Naples, Lee Co., Florida.—On gulf coast, 28 miles below Punta Rassa, reached either via Punta Gorda or Port Tampa; nearest telegraph office at Punta Rassa; tropical climate; good fishing and surf bathing.

C. A. Depuy will give information.
Hotel Naples.—Naples Co., Proprietor; Miss Annie McLaughlin, of Lexington, Kentucky, Manager. Accommodates 100; $3 per day, $15 to $18 per week, $60 to $75 per month; near landing.

Narcoosee, Osceola Co., Florida.—Station on the St. Cloud Sugar Belt Ry., 15 miles from Kissimmee; population of the community, 250; telephone connection.

Nashua, Putnam Co., Florida.—Two miles from Sisco; one-half mile from St. John's River.

Z. H. Dunbar will give information.
Highland House.—Z. H. Dunbar, Proprietor. Accommodates 20; $1.25 per day, $6 per week, $20 per month.

New Cadiz, Hillsboro Co., Florida.—On Boca Ceiga Bay, 4 miles from St. Petersburg; beautifully located on Point Pinallas; bathing and fishing.

Private families will take boarders at reasonable rates.
Address T. Kimball for information.

Newnansville, Alachua Co., Florida.—Station on the S., F. & W. Ry., direct from Savannah; in the midst of a hard-wood and good farming country.

S. T. Prescott will give information.
Red House.—S. T. Prescott, Proprietor. Accommodates 15; 1 mile from the station; $1 per day, $4 per week, $15 per month.

New Orleans, Louisiana.—A Southern city, with a general cosmopolitan appearance, intermingled with distinctively American characteristics; population, 200,000; the Mardi-Gras festivities, which occur on the Tuesday before Ash-Wednesday each year, are famous the world over, and attract visitors from all parts of the world.

From the East, New Orleans is reached via **The Savannah Line** of steamers, and direct rail lines from Savannah.

The hotels and restaurants are as follows:—

St. Charles.—R. E. Rivers, Proprietor. Accommodates 800; St. Charles Street, between Common and Gravier Streets; $4 per day, $28 per week, $120 per month.
City.—R. E. Rivers, Proprietor. Accommodates 700; corner St. Louis and Royal Streets; $2 to $1 per day, $14 to $28 per week, $60 to $100 per month.
Vonderbank.—John Schmitt, Proprietor. Accommodates 175; Magazine Street; $1 to $2 per day.
Cassidy.—M. Cassidy, Proprietor. Accommodates 150; 40 Carondelet Street; $1 per day, $7 per week, $30 per month.
Lafayette.—G. W. Pierce, Proprietor. Accommodates 150; Camp Street; $2 per day, $12 per week, $50 per month.
Denechand.—E. F. Denechand, Proprietor. Accommodates 200; 64 Carondelet Street; $2 per day, $12 per week, $50 per month.
Lalande Flat.—Mrs. Gernon, Proprietor. Accommodates 50; 113 St. Charles Street; $1.25 per day, $15 per week, $60 per month.

THE SAVANNAH LINE IS PREPARED TO

Royal Restaurant.—Nick & Schneider, Proprietors. Accommodates 300; $1.50 per day $8 per week, $25 per month; special orders at reasonable prices.
Leon's Restaurant.—Leon & Lamothe, Proprietors. Accommodates 200; $2 per day, $10 per week, $35 per month; also order meals.
Moreau's Restaurant.—L. Moreau, Proprietor. Special rates, and order meals.
Christian Women's Exchange.—Camp and South Streets. Accommodates 20 to 25; $1.50 per day, $8 per week, $25 per month.
B. J. Martin.—152 Camp Street. Accommodates 25 to 30; $2.50 per day, $15 per week, $60 per month.
Mrs. Bagneta.—168 Julia Street. Accommodates 20 to 30; $1 per day, $5 per week, $20 per month.
Mrs. E. Anderson.—193 Camp Street. Accommodates 10 to 15; $5 to $7 per week, $20 to $25 per month.
Mrs. E. Hollows.—223 Canal Street. Accommodates 25 to 35.
Mrs. C. Herrick.—198 Camp Street. Accommodates 20 to 30; $6 to $8 per week, $25 to $35 per month.
Mrs. Herron.—221 Canal Street. Accommodates 15 to 20; $7 to $8 per week, $25 to $35 per month.
Mr. A. E. Munn.—198 Baronne Street. Accommodates 10 to 20; $5 to $6 per week, $20 to $30 per month.
Mrs. E. C. Cooley.—220 St. Charles Street. $6 per week, $25 to $30 per month.
Mrs. Kittredge.—229 Carondelet Street. Accommodates 20; $10 per week, $25 to $30 per month.
Mrs. Goerts.—241 Baronne Street. Accommodates 12 to 15; $5 per week, $20 per month.
Mrs. J. H. Testard.—256 Baronne Street. Accommodates 15 to 20; $5 per week, $20 per month.
Mrs. McCormack.—159 Carondelet Street. Accommodates 20 to 30; $3 per week, $12 per month. (Rooms only.)
J. C. McAllister.—146 Carondelet Street. Accommodates 20; $5 and upwards per week, $25 per month.
Mrs. Jones.—19 Prytania Street. Accommodates 30; $5 and upward per week, $25 to $35 per month.
Mrs. C. L. Taylor.—223 Carondelet Street. Accommodates 40; $10 per week, $30 to $40 per month.
Mrs. Taffee.—163 Joseph Street. Accommodates 25; $5 and upwards per week, $20 to $25 per month.
Mrs. Sexton.—143 Carondelet Street. Accommodates 50; $5 and upwards per week, $20 to $30 per month.
Mrs. Brown.—144 Camp Street. Accommodates 15; $6 per week, $25 to $35 per month.
Mrs. Gooman.—159 Carondelet Street. Accommodates 22; $6 to $7 per week, $25 per month.
Mrs. Clark.—7 Carondelet Street. Accommodates 20 to 30; $5 to $7 per week, $20 to $30 per month.
Mrs. A. E. Cooley.—220 St. Charles Street. Furnished rooms; $1 to $3 per day.

New River, Bradford Co., Florida.—Station on the G. S. & F. Ry.

R. A. Braughton will give information.

New Smyrna, Volusia Co., Florida.—Station on the Atlantic & Western R. R., also on the Hillsboro River; population of the community about 800; money-order, telegraph, and Southern Express Co.'s office; fishing, hunting, and fine drives.

R. S. Nelson will give information.
Ocean House.—F. W. Sams, Proprietor. Accommodates 150; $3 per day, $15 per week, $60 per month.
Hillsboro House.—Peter Paul, Proprietor. Accommodates 50; $2 per day, special by week or month.

New Upsala, Orange Co., Florida.—(See Upsala.)

HANDLE FREIGHT MORE PROMPTLY THAN OTHERS.

Nocatee, De Soto Co., Florida.—On the C. H. Division of the Florida Southern Ry.; population of the community about 300; Southern Express Co.'s office; 4 miles from Arcadia, which is the nearest telegraph and money-order office.
  Address for information J. R. Windham, Agent, Florida Southern Ry., or E. H. McQuady.

Norwalk, Putnam Co., Florida.—Landing on the St. John's River.
  B. L. Hickman will give information.

Oakdale, Citrus Co., Florida.—Six miles from Homasassa; population of the community about 100; situated at the head of two rivers; abundance of fish and oysters.
  O. P. Blairdell will give information.

Oak Grove, Santa Rosa Co., Florida.—Fifteen miles from Milligan.
  Michael King will give information.

Oak Hill, Volusia Co., Florida.—On Mosquito Lagoon; by steamboat from New Smyrna or Titusville; population of the community, 200; fine hunting and fishing; ducks, deer, snipe, and quail in abundance.
  F. W. Sams will give information.
  Atlantic House.—F. W. Sams, Proprietor. Accommodates 75; $4 per day, $21 per week, $80 per month.

Oakland, Orange Co., Florida.—Station on the Orange Belt Ry., also on the Tavares & Gulf R. R.; population, 300; situated on Lake Apopka; location of the general offices and shops of the Orange Belt Ry.
  T. J. Appleyard will give information.
  Windsor Hotel.—Mrs. L. T. Petris, Proprietor. Near the station; accommodates 75; $2 per day, $10 per week, $30 per month.
  Mrs. E. F. Smith.—(Private boarding-house). Reasonable rates.

Oak Lawn, Dade Co., Florida.—On Lake Worth; reached by way of the Indian River and the J. & L. W. R. R.; 14 miles from Jupiter; beautiful location on Lake Worth, in the midst of cocoanut groves and pineapple fields.
  Oak Lawn House.—A. E. Heyser, Proprietor. Near the steamer landing; accommodates 35; $2 to $2.50 per day, $10 to $12.50 per week, $40 to $50 per month.
  M. A. Heyser will give information.

UNEQUALED FACILITIES.

O'Brien or O'Brine, Suwanee Co., Florida.—Station on the S., F. & W. Ry., 5 miles from Branford.

W. F. Shepherd will give information.

Ocala, Marion Co., Florida.—One of the thriftiest cities in the State; is a station on the Florida Southern Ry. Division of the J., T. & K. W. system, on the Southern Division of the F. C. & P. R. R., and the northern terminus of the S. S., O. & G. R. R., and location of headquarters of the last named; population, 4500; known as "The Brick City;" street cars, electric lights, water-works, and all the conveniences of a city; is the county-seat; Silver Springs only 6 miles distant; in the midst of a fine farming country; numerous old orange and lemon groves; headquarters for some of the most successful and largest phosphate mines in the State.

F. C. Alworth, Ticket Agent, Florida Southern Ry.
John Dozier, Ticket Agent, F. C. & P. R. R.
The **Ocala House.**—The Ocala Co., Owners; E. W. Agnew, Manager. Accommodates 300; $2.50 to $4 per day, special by the week or month.
The **Montezuma.**—Robert Clark, Proprietor. Accommodates 100; $2 to $3 per day, special by the week or month.
Central Hotel.—J. N. Strobar, Owner; Mrs. M. Radcliffe, Manager. Accommodates 60; $2 to $2.50 per day, $8 to $10 per week, $25 per month and upward.
Magnolia Hotel. Mrs. Hooper, Proprietor. Accommodates 50; $2 to $2.50 per day, special by the week or month.
Lancaster's Hotel. Mrs. Lancaster, Proprietor. Accommodates 25; $1.50 per day and upward, special by the week or month.
Brown House.—Mrs. Seth Brown, Proprietor. On Fort King Avenue; accommodates 15; $1.50 per day, $7 to $10 per week.
Vatoldi Restaurant and Boarding-House.—M. A. Harris, Owner; C. C. Harris, Manager; on European or American plans; $2 per day (American), $8 per week (American), $6 per week or $22 per month for meals only, $30 per month for meals and room.
Whitfield House.—Mrs. Whitfield, Proprietor. Accommodates 25; $1.50 per day, $7 to $10 per week.
H. C. Gates.—(Private board).— Corner of Public Square; accommodates 25; $1 per day, $4.50 per week, $18 per month.
Mrs. W. J. McGrath.—Furnished apartments. Accommodates 50; $2.50 to $5 per week.

Ocklawaha River.—A peculiarly beautiful narrow stream, on which the steamers travel from lovely Silver Springs, in Marion Co., to Palatka. The mouth of the river is about 25 miles from Palatka. This stream has a world-wide reputation as a great curiosity.

H. L. Hart, Manager, or R. J. Adams, Agent, Ocklawaha River Nav. Co., Palatka, Florida, will give information.

Ocklockne, Leon Co., Florida.—On the Ocklockne River, 8 miles from Tallahassee.

Ocoee, Orange Co., Florida.—On the Florida Midland Ry., 6 miles from Apopka; population of the community about 250; located in the midst of the Apopka region; numerous orange groves and vegetable farms.

H. K. Clarke or W. C. Roper will give information.
Private board at Minor's, Bigelow's, or Tison's, at $1.50 to $2 per day.

SOUTHERN PRODUCTS TRANSPORTED PROMPTLY.

Oconee, Washington Co., Georgia.—On the main stem of the C. R. R. of Georgia; population of the community, 200; telegraph and Southern Express Co.'s office.
H. B. Joyner, Agent, C. R. R. of Georgia.
Snell House.—H. B. Joyner, Proprietor. $1 per day, $4 per week, $15 per month.

Oglethorpe, Macon Co., Georgia.—On the South-western Division of the C. R. R. of Georgia; population, 900; money-order, telegraph, and Southern Express Co.'s office; fine artesian wells.
The Oglethorpe.—Mrs. G. W. Nelson, Proprietor. Accommodates 60; $1.50 per day, $7 per week, $15 per month and upward.
W. J. Griffen, Agent, C. R. R. of Georgia.

Ohoopee, Tatnall Co., Georgia.—On the main stem of the C. R. R. of Georgia.
A. G. Perdue, Agent, C. R. R. of Georgia.
Cowart Hotel.—G. W. Cowart, Proprietor. About 250 yards from the station; accommodates 30; $1.50 to $3 per day, $15 to $25 per week.

Okahumpka, Lake Co., Florida.—Station on the Florida Southern Ry. Division of the J., T. & K. W. system, 6 miles from Leesburg; in the midst of beautiful clear-water lakes, near the famous Crystal Spring; large kaolin deposit, recently discovered; boating, fishing, and hunting.
Russel W. Bennett, or W. M. Bennett, Agent, Florida Southern Ry., will give information.
The Clarendon.—Joseph Jones, Proprietor. One block from the station; $2 per day, $10 per week.
Mrs. Jeffreys.—Private board at reasonable rates.

Old Town, Lafayette Co., Florida.—On the Suwanee River; by steamer from New Branford; steamer makes two trips per week.
L. C. McCarty.—Private board. One hundred yards from the landing. Accommodates 12; $1 per day, $5 per week, $20 per month.

Olustee, Baker Co., Florida.—Station on the Western Division of the F. C. & P. R. R.; situated on a clear-water lake; population of the community, 400; telegraph and Southern Express Co.'s office.
Chas. H. Baxter or Joseph W. Wood, Agent, F. C. & P. R. R., will give information.
William Lesesne.—Private board. At rates $1 per day, $5 per week, $15 per month.
E. Dyess.—Private board. At rates $1 per day, $5 per week, $15 per month.

Oneco, Manatee Co., Florida.—Four miles from Manatee; population of the community about 100; the Royal Palm Nursery, one of the largest in the South, is located here; in the midst of large orange groves and vegetable farms.
A. A. Saunders will give information.

Orange Bend, Lake Co., Florida.—On the Florida Southern Division of the J., T. & K. W. system, 7 miles from Leesburg; population of the community about 100.
O. F. Baber, Agent, Florida Southern Ry.

Orange City, Volusia Co., Florida.—Station on the Atlantic & Western R. R.; population about 800; 2 miles from Blue Spring, one of the largest springs in the State.
John E. Stillman or S. M. Morse will give information.
Orange City Hotel.—D. Freeman, Proprietor. Accommodates 40; $2 per day, $8 to $10 per week, special by the month.
Deyarman House.—H. H. Deyarman, Proprietor. Accommodates 60; $2 per day, $10 per week.

ALWAYS TRAVEL VIA THE SAVANNAH LINE.

Orange Heights, Alachua Co., Florida.—On the Southern Division of the F. C. & P. R. R.; population of the community about 150; 5 miles from Waldo, 2 miles from Santa Fé Lake.
W. C. Kennedy.—Private board. $1.50 per day, $5 per week.
D. F. Gaylord, Agent, F. C. & P. R. R.

Orange Home, Sumter Co., Florida.—On the Southern Division of the F. C. & P. R. R.; population of the community about 300; situated between two lakes, affording fine fishing and a very attractive location.
Board can be had in private families from $20 to $25 per month.
R. Walpole, Agent, F. C. & P. R. R., will give information.

Orange Park, Clay Co., Florida.—Station on the J., T. & K. W. R. R., also on the St. John's River; population of the community about 300; money-order, telegraph, and Southern Express Co.'s office; beautiful drive along the river bank for 3 miles; good fishing.
Hotel Marion.—E. N. Holt, Proprietor. One mile from the station by carriage; 3 minutes' walk from the steamer landing; accommodates 100; $3 per day, $14 to $21 per week.
W. D. Ball will give information.

Orchard Hill, Spalding Co., Georgia.—Station on the main stem of the C. R. R. of Georgia, 6 miles from Griffin.

Orchid, Brevard Co., Florida.—On the Indian River, near Melbourne; excellent fishing and hunting; surf bathing; ocean 1 mile distant; river dotted with islands.
Frank Forster will give information.

Orlando, Orange Co., Florida.—Station on the South Florida R. R., also on the Southern Division of the F. C. & P. R. R., and the E. F. & A. R. R.; known as "The Phenomenal City," on account of its rapid growth; population, 5000; money-order, telegraph, and Southern Express Co.'s offices; has all the conveniences of a city—paved sidewalks, street railway, city water-works, gas, &c.; the South Florida R. R. has one of the finest passenger stations in the Southern country at this point; in the midst of numerous clear-water lakes, 13 of which can be seen from the top of the market building; in the midst of a fine orange and grape-growing country; is the county-seat; $50,000 court-house now under contract for construction.
W. R. O'Neal, City Ticket Agent, South Florida R. R.
J. A. Clark, Depot Ticket Agent, South Florida R. R.
H. G. Crowder, Freight Agent, South Florida R. R.
W. B. Tucker, General Agent, F. C. & P. R. R.
J. W. Fleming, Ticket Agent, F. C. & P. R. R.
E. E. Ives, Freight Agent, F. C. & P. R. R.
J. H. Abbott, General Manager, E. F. & A. R. R.
San Juan Hotel.—M. P. Courser, Proprietor. Accommodates 135; $3.50 per day, $21 per week, special by the month.
The Arcade.—G. W. Burden, Proprietor; J. D. Burden, Manager. Accommodates 100; $2 per day, $10 to $12 per week, special by the month.
The Magnolia.—Ned Forrest, Proprietor. $2 per day, special by the week or month.
Avenue House.—Mrs. G. Taylor, Proprietor. Accommodates 30; $1.50 per day, special by the week or month.
Cottage Home.—Private board. Mrs. C. J. Miller, Proprietor. Accommodates 24; $1 per day, $6 per week, $25 per month, special rates for the season.
R. C. Knight.—Private board. $8 to $12 per week, $30 to $45 per month.

The Savannah Line Steamers are the finest.

Ormond, Volusia Co., Florida.—(Sometimes written "Ormond-on-the-Halifax"); landing on the Halifax River, and a station on the J., St. A. & H. R. R.; one of the most popular winter resorts in the State; the great attraction of Ormond is its drives and beach—a hard beach, and also drives through hammocks and cultivated lands; steamers from here down the Indian River; ample facilities for sailing, boating, driving, fishing, and hunting.

The Ormond.—The Ormond Hotel Co., Proprietors; Anderson & Price, Managers. Accommodates 275; one-half mile from the railroad station, and one-quarter mile from the steamer landing by horse cars; $1 to $5 per day, $17.50 to $28 per week, $65 to $100 per month; telegraph office and livery; all the conveniences of a first-class hotel; special rates will be made during the month of January and April.

Hotel Coquina.—Ormond Beach Hotel Co., Proprietors; Seiser & Vining, Managers. Accommodates 75; on the ocean beach; $3 per day, $15 to $17.50 per week.

The Sunnyside.—S. A. Penfield, Proprietor. Accommodates 15; $1.50 per day, $8 per week, $30 per month.

Granada.—H. V. Betts, Proprietor. Accommodates 40; $2 per day, $10 per week, $45 per month.

Rose Cottage.—Frank Mason, Proprietor. Accommodates 6; $2 per day, $10 per week, $35 per month.

J. A. Bostrom.—Private board; $10 per week.

Messrs. Anderson and **Price** or **Messrs. Seiser** and **Vining** will give information.

Osprey, Manatee Co., Florida.—On Sarasota Bay; boating, fishing, and bathing.

Webb's Hotel.—John G. Webb, Proprietor. $1.50 per day, $8 per week, $30 per month.

Osteen, Volusia Co., Florida. Station on the J., T. & K. W. R. R.; telegraph and Southern Express Co.'s office; hunting and fishing.

J. A. Blanvelt.—Private board. Accommodates 20; $1.50 per day, $7 per week, $25 per month and upward.

Otter Creek, Levy Co., Florida.—Station on the Cedar Key Division of the F. C. & P. R. R.; population of the community about 100; Southern Express Co.'s and telegraph office; located on the Wacasassa River, near the famous Gulf Hammock; fine hunting and fishing.

G. W. Maxwell or T. J. Yearty will give information.

Otter Creek House.—O. P. H. Kirkland, Proprietor. $2 per day.

Oviedo, Orange Co., Florida.—Station on the S. & I. R. R. Division of the South Florida R. R., also on the E. F. & A. R. R., and on the shores of Lake Jesup; in the centre of some of the largest orange groves in the State.

Messrs. Lee & Todd, or C. D. Crutchfield, Agent, S. F. R. R., will give information.

Cushing House.—F. L. Cushing, Proprietor. Two hundred yards from the station; $2 per day, special rates by the month.

Oviedo House.—T. J. Lawton, Proprietor. One hundred and fifty yards from the station; accommodates 25; $2 per day, $8 per week, $25 per month.

Brewster House.—O. H. Brewster, Proprietor. One hundred and fifty yards from the station; $2 per day, special by the week or month.

Owensboro, Pasco Co., Florida.—Junction of the South Florida R. R. and the F. C. & P. R. R.; population of the community about 100; telegraph and Southern Express Co.'s office.

C. H. Lutz will give information.

UNEQUALED FACILITIES.

ORMOND.

Oxford, Sumter Co., Florida.—Station on the Southern Division of the F. C. & P. R. R., 20 miles from Ocala; population of the community, 700; telegraph and Southern Express Co.'s offices; Lake Miona affords good fishing and boating; good hunting; quail, deer, bear, panther.

J. P. Murdock will give information.
The Pierrepont House.—At rate of $1 per day and upward; special rates for week or month.
City Hotel.—At $1 per day and upward.

Ozark, Dale Co., Alabama.—On the South-western Division of the C. R. R. of Ga., also on the Alabama Midland Ry.; population, 2000; money-order, telegraph, and Southern Express Co.'s office.

W. B. Goodbread will give information.
Speller House.—J. A. Speller, Proprietor. One hundred yards from the station by omnibus; accommodates 50; $2 per day, $8 per week, $25 to $30 per month.
Painter House.—Mrs. L. Knight, Proprietor.
Numerous boarding-houses at reasonable rates.

Ozona, Hillsboro Co., Florida.—On Bay St. Joseph, 6 miles from Tarpon Springs; population of the community about 500.

W. V. Futrell will give information.
Ozona House.—W. V. Futrell, Proprietor. $1 per day, $5 per week, $16 per month and upward.
Eavey House.—L. H. Eavey, Proprietor. $1 per day, $5 per week, $16 per month and upward.
Millard House. Mrs. Millard, Proprietor. $1 per day, $5 per week, $16 per month and upward.

Paisley, Lake Co., Florida.—Seven miles from Altoona.

G. H. Gardiner will give information.
Mrs. William Gardiner.—Private board. $1 per day, $5 per week.

Palatka, Putnam Co., Florida.—On the J., T. & K. W. Ry.; northern terminus of the Florida Southern Ry.; southern terminus of the Georgia Southern & Florida R. R.; landing on St. John's River; population, 3500; all the conveniences of a model city, including street-car lines; hunting and fishing; orange groves; pleasant homes.

H. H. McDonald, Ticket Agent, Union Depot.
Putnam House.—First-class winter hotel. Accommodates 500; $4 per day and upward
St. George.—G. W. Bassett, Proprietor. Accommodates 60; $2 to $4 per day, special by the week or month.
Florida Hotel.—J. H. Carpenter, Proprietor. Accommodates 50; $2 per day, $7 to $10 per week, $28 to $35 per month.
Mrs. M. Devereux.—Private board. Accommodates 15; $2 per day, special by the week or month.
Mrs. E. M. Haughton.—Private board. Accommodates 20; $1.50 to $2 per day, $8 to $10 per week, $30 to $40 per month.

Palermo, St. John's Co., Florida.—On the St. John's River, 8 miles from Green Cove Springs.

A. Esperaudieu will give information.

The Fastest Passenger Steamships

Palm Beach, Dade Co., Florida.—On the east shore of Lake Worth, one-half mile from the Atlantic Ocean; reached by the Indian River and the J. & L. W. Ry.; telephone connection with Jupiter. 16 miles distant; population about 200; there is a yacht club, in which persons can take membership for any length of time; splendid deer, turkey, and duck shooting, boating and fishing.
Walter R. Moore will give information.
Cocoanut Grove House.—E. N. Dimick, Proprietor. Near the landing; accommodates 85; $2.50 to $3.50 per day, $15 to $21 per week, special by the month.
Moore's Cottage.—Mrs. R. B. Moore, Proprietor. Near the landing; accommodates 20; $2 per day, $15 per week and upward.
There are also **Palm Beach Cottage** and **White's Cottage**, both at reasonable rates.

Palmetto, Manatee Co., Florida.—Landing on the Manatee River; population of the community, 500; money-order office; 20 miles from Port Tampa or St. Petersburg; good fishing, hunting, bathing, and boating; very successful in the cultivation of vegetables, oranges, and lemons.
W. E. Parrish will give information.
Palmetto House.—R. D. Stanley, Proprietor. Accommodates 15; $1 per day, $3.50 per week.

Palm Springs, Orange Co., Florida.—Junction of the Florida Midland and the Orange Belt Ry., also on the Wekiva River; population of the community about 300; money-order and Southern Express Co.'s office; nearest telegraph office, Altamonte Springs; 12 large sulphur springs, the largest of which are the Palm Springs and the Hoosier Springs; numerous orange groves.
W. W. Hunt will give information.

Panasoffkee, Sumter Co., Florida.—On the Withlacoochee River; station on the Tampa Division of the F. C. & P. R. R.; population of the community 400; telegraph and Southern Express Co.'s offices; good hunting and fishing.
J. E. Hart, Agent, F. C. & P. R. R., will give information.
The Lake View.—Mrs. J. R. G. Hamilton, Proprietor. Accommodates 50; near the station; $2 per day, special by the week or month.

Paola, Orange Co., Florida.—Station on the S. & L. E. Division of the J., T. & K. W. R. R., also on the Orange Belt Ry.; population of the community, 150; beautiful rolling, high pine land.
J. F. Harrison will give information.
Pine Crest Inn.—On Lake Lillian. W. S. P. Shields, 735 Walnut Street, Philadelphia, Pa., Owner. Accommodates 75 to 100; $10 to $20 per week, special rates by the month or whole season; three-quarters of a mile from the station by carriages.

Parish, Manatee Co., Florida.—Nine miles from Ellenton.

Parkersburgh, Marion Co., Florida.—Located on Blue Springs, 7 miles from Dunellon; population of the community about 150; situated in the midst of several clear-water lakes.
George Hargreaves will give information.
Parkersburgh House.—T. W. Hood, Proprietor. Accommodates 30; $1 per day, $5 per week.

flying the American Flag.

Pasadena, Pasco Co., Florida.—On the F. C. & P. R. R., 3 miles from Dade City; on the shores of Lake Pasadena, a clear-water lake, 12 miles in circumference, affording splendid boating and fishing.

C. E. Spencer will give information.
Lake View Highland.—S. R. Barry, Proprietor; Rev. A. E. Drew, Manager. One and one-half miles from the station by free hack. Accommodates 50; $2 per day, $10 per week, $30 per month.

Pemberton (Pemberton Ferry), Sumter Co., Florida.—Junction of the Florida Southern Ry. Division of the J., T. & K. W. system, and the Pemberton Ferry Branch of the South Florida R. R.; telegraph and South Southern Express Co.'s office; population of the community, 150; fishing and hunting; phosphate mines near by.

J. W. Bishop, Agent, will give information.
Mrs. J. J. Bradford.—Private board. $1.50 per day, $5 per week, $18 per month.
Mrs. McCollum.—Private board. $1.50 per day, $5 per week, $18 per month.

Penn, Putnam Co., Florida.—On the east side of the St. John's River; population of the community about 150; 8 miles from Palatka.

J. M. McCallum will give information.

Peoria, Clay Co., Florida.—Station on the J., T. & K. W. Ry.

W. H. Silcox will give information.

Perry, Houston Co., Georgia.—On the South-western Division of the C. R. R. of Georgia; population of the town and community, 3000; money-order, telegraph, and Southern Express Co.'s office.

Perry Hotel.—J. M. Tuttle, Proprietor. Fifty yards from the station; accommodates 50; $2 per day, $10 per week, $30 per month.
E. M. Fuller, Agent, C. R. R. of Georgia.

Perry's Mill (P. O. name Myrtle), Montgomery Co., Georgia.—On the South-western Division of the C. R. R. of Georgia; population of the community, 150; 12 miles from Montgomery.

S. A. Lide.—(Private boarding-house.) Two hundred yards from the station; $1 per day, $6 per week, $20 per month.

Picolata, St. John's Co., Florida.—On the St. John's River; population of the community about 200; 12 miles from Green Cove Springs.

Montgomery Corse will give information.

Pierson, Volusia Co., Florida.—Station on the J., T. & K. W. R. R.; population of the community about 200; high, rolling pine lands; numerous fine orange groves.

N. L. Pierson will give information.
N. L. Pierson.—(Private board.) $1 per day, $6 per week, $20 per month.

Pinecastle, Orange Co., Florida.—Station on the South Florida R. R., 5 miles from Orlando; population of the community, 300.

Isaac Aten will give information.
Sweet House.—Two hundred yards from the station; accommodates 10.

TICKETS INCLUDE MEALS AND BERTH.

Pine Level, De Soto Co., Florida.—Nine miles from Arcadia; one-quarter mile to fishing ground and 2 miles to deer and wild turkey range.

Private boarding-houses; $1.50 per day, $15 per month and upward.
Joseph Mizell will give information.

Plant City, Hillsboro Co., Florida.—Crossing of main line of the South Florida R. R. and the Tampa Division of the F. C. & P. R. R.; population of the town and neighborhood, 1200; money-order, telegraph, and Southern Express Co.'s offices; good hunting, quail, deer, and small game; fine orange groves; very productive locality.

H. H. Dickey, Agent, South Florida R. R.
R. H. Willie, Agent, F. C. & P. R. R.
Tropical Hotel.—L. D. Green, Proprietor. Accommodates 200; $2 per day, $5 per week and upward.
Robinson House.—J. B. Robinson, Proprietor. Accommodates 100; $2 per day, $5 per week and upward.
Private boarding-houses at $3.50 per week and upward.

Plymouth, Orange Co., Florida.—Station on the Southern Division of the F. C. & P. R. R.; population of the community about 50; 5 miles from Apopka; telegraph and Southern Express Co.'s office.

W. A. Chapman, Agent, F. C. & P. R. R.
Lake Standish House.—H. E. Smith, Proprietor. One-half mile from the station; accommodates 60; $12 to $20 per week.

Pomona, Putnam Co., Florida.—Station n the J., T. & K. W. Ry.; population about 100; money-order, telegraph, and Southern Express Co.'s office; lake 2 miles in circumference; fine fishing and boating; church and school-house; several good orange groves.

J. H. Eames will give information.
Ames House.—T. Ames, Proprietor; G. H. A. Fisk, Manager. Accommodates about 20 $1.50 and $2 per day, $9 to $12 per week, $30 to $40 per month.

Ponce Park, Volusia Co., Florida.—On the Halifax River, 5 miles from New Smyrna; fishing and hunting; surf bathing and boating of all kinds; fine hard beach for driving.

La Ponce Hotel.—E. C. Rogers, Proprietor. Accommodates 50; $3 per day, $12 to $15 per week, $30 to $40 per month.
Pacetti House.—B. C. Pacetti, Proprietor. Accommodates 20; $7 to $10 per week; also furnished cottages ready for occupancy.
N. Hasty will give information.

Port Orange, Volusia Co., Florida.—On the Halifax River, 5 miles from Daytona.

Port Orange House.—A. Brohm, Proprietor. Near the landing; accommodates 50; $2 per day, $8 per week.

Port Tampa, Hillsboro Co., Florida.—The southern deep-water terminus of the Plant system, and, with the rapid development of trade with South America and the West India Islands, the export trade of phosphate to Europe has become a centre of great activity;

THE FASTEST PASSENGER STEAMSHIPS

only point on the Gulf having 24 feet of water. In order to provide a convenient place for passengers to await the departure of trains and steamers there has been erected on the pier The Inn,—a unique structure with every convenience, richly furnished, and complete in every detail, of service. The surrounding waters teem with fish, while ducks, pelicans, and gulls circle about overhead. Facilities for boating and bathing are at hand.

The Inn.—Plant Investment Co., Proprietors; C. E. Hoadley, Manager. Accommodates 100; strictly first-class hotel; $4 to $5 per day, $28 to $35 per week.

Port Tampa City (P. O. at Port Tampa), Hillsboro Co., Florida.— On Tampa Bay, and also a station on the South Florida R. R.; population about 300; telegraph and Southern Express Co.'s office; a rapidly-growing new city on the bay.

The Pines.—George Newell, Proprietor. Accommodates 35; $2 per day, $10.50 per week, $30 per month; one-quarter mile from the station.

C. E. Hoadley, Port Tampa, will give information.

Punta Gorda, De Soto Co., Florida.—Southern terminus of the C. H. Division of the Florida Southern Ry., on the Charlotte Harbor; justly celebrated as a great resort of sportsmen, especially fishers.

The Punta Gorda.—William A. Warden, Proprietor. Accommodates 400; $3 per day and upward; beautifully-located hotel on the bay.

Putnam, Marion Co., Georgia.—On the S. & W. Division of the C. R. R. of Ga.; population of the community, 300.

P. S. Stephens.—Private board. Accommodates 20; $1.50 per day, $5 per week, $15 per month; near the station.

Putnam Hall, Putnam Co., Florida.—One mile from Putnam Hall station, on the G. S. & F. Ry., 20 miles from Palatka.

L. B. Padgett will give information.

FLYING THE AMERICAN FLAG.

Quincy (county-seat), **Gadsden Co., Florida.**—Station on the Western Division of the F. C. & P. R. R., also 6 miles from Faceville, Ga., S., F. & W. Ry.; population of the community, 1500; money-order, telegraph, and Southern Express Co.'s offices; high, rolling land, very productive; centre of the tobacco-growing district, where Cuba tobacco is being successfully cultivated; The Owl Cigar Co. (Messrs. Stratton & Storm), of New York, have a large tobacco plantation near by, and also plant for the manufacture of cigars.

T. L. Cauley, Agent, F. C. & P. R. R.
The Exchange.—Mrs. F. W. Love, Proprietor. Accommodates 50; $1.50 to $2 per day, $8 to $10 per week, $25 to $30 per month.

Quitman, Brooks Co., Georgia.—Station on the S., F. & W. Ry., 175 miles from Savannah; population, 2500; money-order, telegraph, and Southern Express Co.'s offices; a pretty city; wide streets; fine natural drainage; large oaks and magnolias.

J. G. McCall, or J. T. Davis, Agent, S., F. & W. Ry., will give information.
Hotel Marie, Quitman Hotel Co., Owner; Edward A. Elder, Manager. (Summer address, Indian Springs, Georgia.) Accommodates 150; $2 per day, $8 to $10 per week, $25 per month.
Hotel Main.—S. H. Griffin, Proprietor.
Commercial House.

Reddick, Marion Co., Florida.—Station on the Florida Southern Ry. Division of the J., T. & K. W. system; population of the community about 200; telegraph and Southern Express Co.'s office.

W. P. Ellett, Agent, Florida Southern Ry.

Reynolds, Taylor Co., Georgia.—On the South-western Division of the C. R. R. of Georgia; population of the town and community about 1000; telegraph and Southern Express Co.'s office.

C. B. Marshall, Agent, Central R. R.
Hodgers House.—Mrs. H. Hodgers, Proprietor. One hundred yards from the station; accommodates 40; $1.50 per day, $6 per week, $20 per month.
Paris House.—F. F. Paris, Proprietor. One hundred yards from station; accommodates 25; $1.50 per day, $6 per week, $20 per month.

Richland, Pasco Co., Florida.—On the Pemberton Ferry Branch of the South Florida R. R.; population of the community, 150; telegraph and Southern Express Co.'s office; good fishing and hunting; Withlacoochee River 2 miles distant; Hillsboro River 4 miles distant.

J. D. Redding, Agent, South Florida R. R.
Gill House.—Dr. M. R. Gill, Proprietor. Three hundred yards from the station; accommodates 10; $2 per day, $6 per week, $20 per month.

Ridgewood, Putnam Co., Florida.—Two miles from Welaka; 4 miles from Pomona; population of the community about 50.

G. C. Butler will give information.

UNEQUALED FACILITIES.

Riverland, Hernando Co., Florida.—Station on the Orange Belt Ry.; population of the community about 100.
S. R. A. Kemp will give information.
The Rucker.—W. H. Rucker, Proprietor.

Rochelle, Alachua Co., Florida.—Junction of the main line and Gainesville Branch of Florida Southern Ry. Division of the J., T. & K. W. Ry.; population of the community about 500; telegraph and Southern Express Co.'s office.
J. R. Dewy, Agent, Florida Southern Ry.

Rock Ledge, Brevard Co., Florida.—On the Indian River. A famous resort in the midst of beautiful orange groves; population of the community about 500; money-order, telegraph, and Southern Express Co.'s office.
E. L. McGruder will give information.
Hotel Indian River.—Near the steamer landing. A. S. Lee, Manager. Accommodates 700; first class in every particular; $1 per day and upward, special by the week or month.
Rock Ledge Hotel.
Tropical Hotel.
Wilkinson's Cottages.

Rosewood, Levy Co., Florida.—Station on the Cedar Key Division of the F. C. & P. R. R., 10 miles from Cedar Keys; population of the community about 50.
Ford House.—S. C. Corson, Proprietor. Accommodates 25; very reasonable rates.

Runnymede, Osceola Co., Florida.—On Lake East Tohopekiliga, 2 miles from Narcoosee; good vegetable, sugar, and rice growing region; good hunting and fishing.
Allen Thomas will give information.
The Hotel Runnymede.—At reasonable rates.

Rutland, Sumter Co., Florida.—Landing on the Withlacoochee River, 11 miles from Panasoffkee.
William O. Johnson will give information.

Rutledge, Alachua Co., Florida.—Six miles from Gainesville; population of the community about 100; Warren's Cave 4 miles distant; the "Devil's Mill Hopper," a natural well, 200 feet deep, with almost perpendicular sides, and a lake in the bottom, 1 mile distant.
J. H. Van Deveer will give information.

St. Andrew's (or St. Andrew's Bay), Washington Co., Florida. On the north-east shore of St. Andrew's Bay. Population of the community about 1000; 50 miles from Chipley, Florida. St. Andrew's Bay is a body of water 2 to 5 miles wide, with 3 arms, about 60 miles in length; good boating, bathing, and fishing; good hunting, deer, turkey, quail, geese, and ducks.
J. E. Boren will give information.
Wilson House.—Mrs. J. W. Wilson, Proprietor. One-half block from the landing; accommodates 25; $1 to $2 per day, $6 per week, $20 per month.
Hunt's.—Mrs. C. M. Hunt, Proprietor. Three blocks from the steamer landing; $1 to $2 per day, $5 per week, $20 per month.
St. Andrew's Hotel. Accommodates 75. Will be open this winter.

THE SAVANNAH LINE IS PREPARED TO

St. Augustine, St. John's Co., Florida.—Station on the Jacksonville, St. Augustine & Halifax River Ry.; population, 5000; all the conveniences of a modern city; probably the greatest resort in the world; the oldest town in the United States; many relics of its Spanish days of the sixteenth century—the old city wall and gates; Fort Marion, erected in 1620, still remains; cathedral; old slave-market: the Plaza; the Memorial Presbyterian Church; the sea-wall; Anastasia light-house, 165 feet high; coquina quarries; U. S. barracks; good fishing, boating, and hunting; splendid drives; the Casino, with its wonderfully complete baths; as to hotels, none in the world excel those at St. Augustine; complete livery and omnibus transfer.

W. D. Allen, Ticket Agent, Union Depot; **F. J. Ballard,** Ticket Agent, Ponce De Leon or St. Augustine Improvement Co., will give information.

The Ponce De Leon is one of the finest hotels in the world; in fact, none excel it anywhere. Built in the style of the early Spanish renaissance, strongly influenced by the Moorish spirit, "The eye travels from the gateway in the centre of the one-story portico up to the corner turrets of the wings, then back to the high walls of the main building and up to the great dome, surmounted by its graceful lantern, and so on and up to the huge corner towers that rise one hundred and fifty feet into the clear, blue sky." The material is a shell composite, of a light mother-of-pearl color, ornamented with terra cotta. The loggias overhang the different façades, with their quaint woodwork worn, resembling somewhat the houses in the old town.

In speaking of the construction of this hotel, the word *built* would be improper,—it was *cast*,—the shell and cement being poured in a mould while soft, and rammed into proper position within its mould. The courts are the most beautiful and tastily arranged gardens of flowers, evergreens, walks, fountains, and, in fact, recall all the stories of childhood days of "good fairies" and their abodes. The interior, with its complete and elegant finish, lavish display of the very finest works of art, is beyond description in the small space at command here. To quote a friend, "Think of all the wonderfully beautiful things you have read, heard, or dreamed of, then see the 'Ponce,' and you will say 'its more than that.'" H. M. Flagler, Owner; O. D. Seavey, Manager. Accommodates 700; $5 per day and upward.

Alcazar.—H. M. Flagler, Owner; O. D. Seavey, Manager; B. W. Angell, Superintendent Accommodates 300; on European or American plan.

Cordova.—H. M. Flagler, Owner; E. N. Wilson, Manager. Accommodates 100; $4 to $5 per day, $28 to $42 per week.

San Marco.—J. S. Cruft, Owner; Ainslie & McGilloray, Managers. Accommodates 400; $4 per day and upward, special by the week or month.

Florida House.—Charles F. Beck, Proprietor. Accommodates 200; $3 to $4 per day, special by the week or month.

Magnolia.—W. W. Palmer, Proprietor. Accommodates 250; $3 to $4 per day, special by the week or month.

St. George.—C. D. Tyler, Proprietor. Accommodates 100; $3.50 to $4 per day, special by the week or month.

Ocean View.—W. S. M. Pinkham, Proprietor. Accommodates 75; $2 per day, $10 to $11 per week, $35 to $50 per month.

The Abbey.—W. G. Warden, Owner; Mrs. A. B. Abbe, Proprietor. Accommodates 60; $2 per day, special by the week or month.

Columbia Hotel.—A. S. Washburne, Proprietor. Accommodates 100; $2 per day, $10 to $15 per week.

American House.—W. H. Woodall, Proprietor. Accommodates 40; $2 per day, $7 to $10 per week, $30 to $40 per month.

Villa Oriole.—Accommodates 20. $1.50 per day, $8 to $12 per week, $30 to $50 per month.

La Posada.—Mrs. H. A. Rumley, Proprietor. Accommodates 60; $1.50 to $2 per day, $7 to $10 per week, $30 per month.

Valencia.—Mrs. Frazier, Proprietor. Accommodates 100; $2.50 per day, special by the week or month.

Barcelona.—Miss Hazeltine, Proprietor. Accommodates 50; $2.50 per day, $12 to $18 per week, special by the month.

HANDLE FREIGHT MORE PROMPTLY THAN OTHERS.

Craddock.—Mrs. Craddock, Proprietor. Accommodates 40; $1.50 per day, $8 to $10 per week, special by the month.
Hernandez House.—H. E. Hernandez, Proprietor. Accommodates 40; $1.50 to $2 per day, $7 to $10 per week, $28 to $40 per month.

St. Catherine (or Dragem Junction), Sumter Co., Florida.—Junction of the Florida Southern Ry. Division of the J., T. & K. W. Ry. and the Tampa Division of F. C. & P. R. R.

J. E. Berwick, Agent, Florida Southern Ry.
J. J. Bradford, Agent, F. C. & P. R. R.

St. Cloud, Osceola Co., Florida.—Station on the St. C. S. B. Ry.; population of the community, 350; 7 miles from Kissimmee; in the midst of the celebrated sugar and rice country of Florida.

St. Francis (known as Old Town), Lake Co., Florida.—Landing on the western bank of the St. John's River; population of the community about 100; evidently been a settlement during the days of the Spaniards; located 40 miles above Sanford.

John E. Harris will give information.
Hotel St. Francis.—Dr. L. H. Harris, Proprietor; John E. Harris, Manager. Accommodates 35; $2 per day, $12 per week, $35 per month; near the landing.

St. James City, Lee Co., Florida.—Located on Pine Island, on Charlotte Harbor; reached by the steamer from Punta Gorda or Port Tampa; 4 miles from Punta Rassa; fine tarpon fishing, and small fish in abundance; good hunting.

J. M. Kreamer or E. Whiteside will give information.
San Carlos Hotel.—St. James-on-the-Gulf Co., Proprietors. Accommodates 100; $2.50 to $5 per day, special by the week or month; about one-eighth of a mile from the landing by herdic.

St. Lucie, Brevard Co., Florida.—On the west bank of the Indian River, 2 miles from Fort Pierce; population of the community about 300; good fishing; deer and other game in abundance.

The St. Lucie.—James Paine, Manager. Two hundred yards from the station. Accommodates 30; $3.50 per day, $18 per week.
James Paine, Agent, I. R. S. B. Co.

St. Petersburg, Hillsboro Co., Florida.—Terminus of the Orange Belt Ry., on Tampa Bay; population, 500; money-order, telegraph, and Southern Express Co.'s office; fine fishing, boating, and bathing in the waters of the bay.

S. P. Hollinrake, Agent, Orange Belt Ry.
Hotel Detroit.—C. W. Laud, Proprietor. Near the railroad station; one-half mile from the steamer landing. Accommodates 100; $2.50 to $3.50 per day, $15 to $20 per week, $40 to $75 per month.
Several boarding-houses at reasonable rates.

St. Simon's Mills (better known as St. Simon's Island), Glynn Co., Georgia.—An island in the Atlantic Ocean, near Brunswick.

Ocean View House.—A. T. Arnold, Proprietor. Three-quarter mile from the landing in hack; $1.50 to $2 per day, $9 to $10 per week.

Southern Products Transported Promptly.

The Cordova

The Alcazar

San Antonio, Pasco Co., Florida.—Station on the Orange Belt Ry.; population of the community about 200; money-order, telegraph, and Southern Express Co.'s office.

Florida House,—Joseph Freeze, Proprietor. Accommodates 100; one-half mile from the station by buggy; special rates by the week or month.
Pasco House,—Geo. J. Frese, Proprietor. Accommodates 20; one-quarter mile from station; $2 per day, $8 per week, $30 per month and upward.
Jacob Godwin or J. M. Jones, Agents, Orange Belt Ry., will give information.

Sanford, Orange Co., Florida.—Station on the main stem of the J., T. & K. W. Ry., the South Florida R. R., also northern terminus of the Orange Belt Ry.; landing on the St. John's River; at head of navigation for large steamers. Lake Monroe, a clear-water lake, 6 miles wide; population, 2500; in the midst of a fine orange section; one of the oldest orange groves in the State near by; all the conveniences of a city; money-order, telegraph, and Southern Express Co.'s office; location of general offices of South Florida R. R.; water-works and gas-works; business portion of the city mostly substantial brick buildings; good boating and fishing.

C. R. Walker, Union Ticket Agent, will give information.
Sanford House.—A. B. Hale, Proprietor. Accommodates 300; $4 per day, special by the week or month.
South Florida Sanitarium,—W. A. Miller, Manager. Five blocks from the station; accommodates 65; $2.50 to $4 per day, $15 to $25 per week, $50 to $75 per month.
Comfort Cottage.—Mrs. E. M. Martin, Proprietor. Six blocks from the station; accommodates 30; $2 per day, $12 per week.
Sirrene House.—Mrs. Sirrene, Proprietor. Seven blocks from the station; accommodates 30; $2 to $4 per day, $15 per week.
Pico Restaurant.—South Florida R. R. Co., Owners. Near the station; the dining-room will accommodate 50; rooms will accommodate 14; $2.50 per day.
San Leon Hotel.—A. C. Martin, Proprietor. Seven blocks from the station; accommodates 25.
Florida House.—Mrs. Shelby, Proprietor. Three blocks from the station; accommodates 22; $1.50 per day, $5 per week.
Gate City Boarding-House.—J. H. Ferguson, Proprietor. Two blocks from the station; accommodates 18; $1.50 per day, $5 to $8 per week.

San Mateo, Putnam Co., Florida.—Landing on the St. John's River, 5 miles from Palatka; population of the community, 400; some of the oldest orange groves in the State near by.

D. S. Tingley will give information.
Stanton House.—Mrs. W. E. Stanton, Proprietor. Accommodates 20; $1.50 to $2 per day, $6 to $10 per week, special by the month; 1½ miles from the landing by hotel carriage.
Tiffany House.—E. C. Tiffany, Proprietor. Accommodates 20; $1.50 to $2 per day, $6 to $10 per week, special by the month; near the steamer landing.

Santos, Marion Co., Florida.—Station on the Southern Division of the F. C. & P. R. R., 8 miles from Ocala; population of the community, 200; Southern Express Co.'s office.

C. H. Mathews.—Private board. $1 per day, $5 per week.
Geo. G. Mathews, Jr., will give information.

THE FASTEST PASSENGER STEAMSHIPS

Sarasota, Manatee Co., Florida.—On Sarasota Bay; nearest landing, Braidentown, 12 miles distant; thence by hack; population of the community about 200; boating, fishing, and hunting; sea shells.
J. Hamilton Gillispie will give information.
The De Soto Hotel.—J. Hamilton Gillispie, Proprietor. Accommodates 50; $3 per day, $15 per week.
Sarasota House.—Mrs. Rosie Vincent, Proprietor. Accommodates 15; $2 per day, $10 per week.

Satsuma, Putnam Co., Florida.—On the St. John's River, 2 miles from Satsuma Heights; population of the community, 100; private board at reasonable rates.
Horace Welles will give information.

Satsuma Heights, Putnam Co., Florida.—Station on the J., T. & K. W. Ry.; population of the community, 250; telegraph and Southern Express Co.'s office; one-quarter mile from a large lake; private boarding-houses at reasonable rates.
H. B. Jarvis or E. E. Cardell will give information.

Seaside, Hillsboro Co., Florida.—On the Gulf of Mexico, and also a station on the Orange Belt Ry.; population of the community about 100; 4 miles from Tarpon Springs; surf bathing, fishing, and sailing; lithia, iron, and sulphur springs.
John D. Green, Agent, will give information.
Buchler House.—R. E. Buchler, Proprietor. Accommodates 10; $2 per day, $7 per week, $25 per month; one-quarter mile from the station by team.

Sebastapol, Burke Co., Georgia.—Station on the main stem of the C. R. R. of Ga.
J. P. Jorden, Agent, C. R. R. of Ga.

FLYING THE AMERICAN FLAG.

Savannah, Chatham Co., Georgia.—On the Savannah River, 18 miles from its mouth; a thriving city of 60,000 inhabitants; the most important seaport on the South Atlantic coast; headquarters and southern terminus of **The Savannah Line,** from which port its steamers leave and arrive nearly every day in the week; four each week (Mondays, Wednesdays, Fridays, and Saturdays), leaving for New York—one every four days for Boston direct; one every ten days (for freight) for Philadelphia; visitors are always welcome to inspect the great wharves, docks, and steamers of this Company. Savannah is also the southern terminus of the main stem of the Central R. R. of Georgia. The Central R. R. and **The Savannah Line** being operated by the same system,—the Richmond & Danville R. R. system,—their relation is necessarily very close, the Central R. R. with its own lines radiating from Savannah throughout Georgia, and, with its connections, forming through direct lines throughout the South. Savannah is also the headquarters of the Savannah, Florida & Western Ry. (the Plant system), whose own lines reach all Florida points, and form the U. S. Mail Route to Cuba. At this great port the Central R. R. of Georgia, and also the Savannah, Florida & Western Ry. (the Plant system), find an outlet to the North and East and the foreign ports of the world.

The general business, especially in cotton, lumber, and naval stores, is immense, and ample capital is at hand to handle this great volume of business, which is annually increasing.

Savannah, on account of its superior natural advantages (see page 8), and its ample hotel facilities, is now one of the great winter resorts of this country.

The office of the Ocean Steamship Company, "Savannah Line," is at No. 3 Wardburg Building, foot of Bull Street; C. G. Anderson is the Agent.

The **De Soto** (new), corner of Liberty and Bull Streets, one of the finest and most complete hotels in the world; first class in every particular. Watson & Powers, Proprietors. Accommodates 500; $4 per day and upward; special rates by the week, month, or season.

The **Pulaski House,** corner of Bull and Bryan Streets. Accommodates 200; $2.50 per day and upward.

Screven House, corner Bull and Congress Streets. Accommodates 250; $2.50 per day and upward; special by week or month.

Marshall House, Broughton Street, between Abercomb and Drayton. Accommodates

Harnett House.—M. L. Harnett, Proprietor. Accommodates 150; $2 to $2.50 per day; $10 per week, $30 to $35 per month.

The **Morrison House,** corner Broughton and Drayton Streets. Accommodates 75; $1.50 to $2 per day, $7 to $12 per week, $30 to $40 per month.

Savannah Restaurant, West Broad and Congress Streets. Mrs. E. F. Monroe, Proprietor. Accommodates 50; $1 per day, $5 per week, $20 per month.

Palmer House, 67 Jefferson Street. Mrs. Addie Palmer, Proprietor. Accommodates 15; $1 per day, $5 per week.

First class private board by **Miss E. McAlpin,** No. 68 South Broad Street. Accommodates 35; $2 to $4 per day, $10 to $20 per week.

All hotels easily reached by Feely's Transfer Stages, which are in attendance, upon arrival of all trains or steamers, or by street cars.

UNEQUALED FACILITIES.

THE DE SOTO, SAVANNAH, GA.

Sebastian, Brevard Co., Florida.—On the Indian River; hunting, fishing, bathing, and boating; river 3 miles wide; only a few yards to the Atlantic.

S. Kitching, Agent, I. R. S. B. Co.
S. Kitching.—Private board; 200 yards from the landing; accommodates 10; $1.50 per day, $7 per week, $20 per month.

Seffner, Hillsboro Co., Florida.—On the S. F. R. R., 12 miles from Tampa; population of the community about 300; telegraph, money-order, and Southern Express Company's office; in the midst of a very fertile country; 2 churches; good schools.

N. M. McLaren, Agent, South Florida R. R.
The Seffner House.—Mrs. J. D. Carn, Proprietor. Three minutes' walk from the station; accommodates 50; $1.50 per day, $6 per week, $25 per month.
Oak Crescent.—Mrs. H. C. Ferris, Proprietor. Near the station; accommodates 80; $2 per day, special by the week or month.

Selman, Calhoun Co., Florida.—On the Apalachicola River, 2 miles from the landing; 15 miles from Sneads.

R. F. Shields will give information.

Seminole, Hillsboro Co., Florida.—On Boca Ceiga Bay, 8 miles from Largo; fine surf bathing, and beautiful bay for boating and fishing.

A. P. Hoffman will give information.
Killen Grove House.—F. E. Grable, Proprietor. Accommodates 10; $2 per day, $10 per week, $30 per month.

Senoia, Coweta Co., Georgia.—Station on the main stem of the C. R. R. of Georgia; population, 800; money-order, telegraph, and Southern Express Company's office; in the midst of good, high farming country.

Barnes House.—Miss Sallie Herd, Proprietor; and the
Graham House.—James Graham, Proprietor. Near the station; $1.50 per day, $5 per week, $15 per month.
T. N. Vining, Agent, C. R. R. of Georgia.

Seven Oaks (same as **Bay View**), **Hillsboro Co., Florida.**

Seville, Volusia Co., Florida.—Station on the J., T. & K. W. Ry.; population of the community, 200; money-order, telegraph, and Southern Express Company's office; situated on Lake Louise; has regular city sewerage and water-works; fine orange groves; good boating, hunting, and fishing.

Wm. A. Lecke or W. C. B. Lawson, Agent, J., T. & K. W. Ry., will give information.
The Seville.—Mason Young, Owner. Accommodates 100; $2.50 per day and upward.
Grand View.—H. Singer, Proprietor. $2 per day and upward.

Sharon, Clay Co., Florida.—Station on the Western Ry. of Florida, 10 miles from Green Cove Springs; population of the community about 300; high, rolling pine country.

J. J. Moody will give information.
Humbert House.—Mrs. J. W. Fogleman, Proprietor. $1 per day, $1.50 per week, $15 per month and upward.

THE SAVANNAH LINE IS PREPARED TO

Sharpsburgh, Coweta Co., Georgia.—Station on the main stem of the C. R. R. of Ga.; population, 400; in the midst of a good farming country.

Several private boarding-houses at reasonable rates.

H. H. Harrison, Agent, C. R. R. of Ga.

Shell Creek, De Soto Co., Florida.—Flag station on the Charlotte Harbor Division of the Florida Southern Ry., 3 miles from Cleveland.

Shiloh, Volusia Co., Florida.—Fifteen miles from Titusville, between the head of the Indian River and Mosquito Lagoon.

Silver Pond, Putnam Co., Florida.—Three miles from Denver; 5 miles from Crescent City.

A. J. Spencer will give information.

Silver Springs, Marion Co., Florida.—Station on the Southern Division of the F. C. & P. R. R., 6 miles from Ocala; the Silver Springs are celebrated wherever Florida is known,—a body of water so clear that objects are visible at a depth of over 60 feet; this is the starting point of steamers on the Ocklawaha River.

James Coons will give information.
Silver Springs Hotel.—Proskey Bros., Proprietors. Summer address, Bellport, L. I. Accommodates 100; $3 to $4 per day, $16 to $18 per week.

Silver Springs Park (P. O. name **Springs Park**), **Marion Co., Florida.**—Station on the Southern Division of the F. C. & P. R. R.; population of the community, 500; 2 miles from the celebrated Silver Springs.

L. M. Wilson will give information.
Hotel Marion.—Frank M. Brown, Proprietor. Accommodates 50; $2 per day, special by the week or month.

Sisco, Putnam Co., Florida.—Station on the J., T. & K. W. Ry., 3 miles from Pomona; population of the community about 150.

H. V. Sisco, Agent, J., T. & K. W. Ry.
C. C. Bartlett.—Private board. Near the station. $1.50 per day, $7 per week, special by the month.

Smith's Creek, Wakulla Co., Florida.—On the Ocklocknee River, 30 miles from St. Mark's; population of the community about 150.

J. B. Langston will give information.

Sneads, Jackson Co., Florida.—Station on the Pensacola & Atlantic R. R., 3 miles from Apalachicola River; population, 500; plenty of fish, deer, turkey, quail, and squirrels.

W. F. Jenkins will give information.
Boykin House.—Mrs. J. C. Boykin, Proprietor. Accommodates 30; $1.50 per day, $5 to $7 per week.
Solomon's Hotel.—J. Z. Solomon, Proprietor. Accommodates 30; $1.50 per day, $5 to $7 per week.

HANDLE FREIGHT MORE PROMPTLY THAN OTHERS.

Sorrento, Lake Co., Florida.—Station on the S. & L. E. Division of the J., T. & K. W. Ry., 6 miles from Sanford; population of the community about 300; high, rolling pine land; numerous springs; money-order and Southern Express Co.'s office.

A. S. Matlack, Agent, J., T. & K. W. Ry.
Averill House.—Dr. W. F. Thomas, Proprietor. Accommodates 20; $2 per day, $7 per week; one-quarter mile from the station.

South Lake Weir, Marion Co., Florida.—Station on the Florida Southern Ry. Division of the J., T. & K. W. system; on the shores of Lake Weir; 20 miles from Ocala; population of the community about 300; Lake Weir is one of the prettiest lakes in the State, on the shores of which are many fine orange groves; good fishing and hunting.

Wm. Foster or P. O. Hawthorne will give information.
Lakeside Hotel.—E. B. Foster, Proprietor; T. B. Shay, Manager. Accommodates 60; $2 to $3 per day; special by the week or month; one-quarter mile from the station by hack.
Amaskohegan House.—J. H. Albeston, Proprietor. Accommodates 15; $1 per day, $6 per week, $20 per month; 3 miles from the station; will meet train or steamer upon notice.
Arnold House.—M. J. Arnold, Proprietor. Accommodates 15; $1 to $2 per day, $7 to $12 per week; one-half mile from the station by hack.

Spring Garden, Volusia Co., Florida.—One and one-quarter miles from De Leon Springs; population, 100.

Argyle Hotel—A. H. Norris, Owner. (Summer address, Morganville, N. Y.) Miss Carrie Douglas, Manager. Accommodates 25; at reasonable rates; 1¼ miles from the railroad station by Jersey wagon.

Spring Lake, Clay Co., Florida.—Station on the Western Ry. of Florida.

A. M. Williams will give information.

Spring Glen (P. O. name St. Nicholas), Duval Co., Florida.— On Jacksonville & Atlantic R. R. and Little Arlington River, 3 miles from Jacksonville.

Spring Glen House.—Mrs. E. Clute, Proprietor. (Summer address, Sheepshead Bay N. Y.) Accommodates 25; $2 per day, $8 to $10 per week.

Starke (county-seat of), Bradford Co., Florida.—Station on the Southern Division of the F. C. & P. R. R.; population, 1000; money-order, telegraph, and Southern Express Company's offices; quite a distributing point; fine lakes and good fishing near by; in the heart of the strawberry region; many flourishing orange groves.

S. F. Gardner or J. P. Hester, Agent, will give information.
Commercial Hotel.—J. Kleinschmidt, Proprietor. Accommodates 50; $2 per day, $7 per week and upward; special monthly rates.
Kentucky House.—J. R. Martin, Proprietor. Accommodates 30; $2 per day, $7 per week and upward.
Starke House.—Mrs. F. B. Jones, Proprietor. Accommodates 20; $2 per day, $7 per week and upward.

Steinhatchie (Cook's Hammock), Lafayette Co., Florida.— Twenty-five miles from Branford.

J. W. Grau will give information.

TICKETS INCLUDE MEALS AND BERTH.

Stockton (or Fairview), Marion Co., Florida.—On the Withlacoochee River, 8 miles from Leroy.
A. McC. Brass will give information.

Summerfield, Marion Co., Florida.—Station on the Southern Division of the F. C. & P. R. R.; population of the community, 150; telegraph and Southern Express Company's office.
O. D. Smith, Agent, F. C. & P. R. R.
Dillard's House.—S. N. Dillard, Proprietor. One hundred yards from the station; accommodates 15; $1.50 per day, $5 per week, $18 per month.

Summit, Marion Co., Florida.—On the Florida Southern Railway Division of the J., T. & K. W. system, 5 miles from Altoona; Southern Express Company's office; large boiling spring, makes a stream large enough to float a steamboat; several clear-water lakes; good hunting and fishing; deer, bear, and wild turkeys.
O. L. Baber, Agent, Florida Southern Ry., or Lewis L. Clark, will give information.
Lewis L. Clark.—Private board; accommodates 10; $1 per day, $3.50 per week.

Sumner, Levy Co., Florida.—Seven miles from Cedar Key.
J. P. Little will give information.
Hudson House.—J. B. Hudson, Proprietor. $1.50 per day, $6 per week and upward.

Sumterville, Sumter Co., Florida.—Station on the Tampa Division of the F. C. & P. R. R., 2 miles from Panasoffkee; population of the community about 200; numerous curious sinks and natural wells abound in this vicinity; vegetable and orange growing country.
H. T. Mann will give information.
Warren House.—John T. Warren, Proprietor. Three hundred yards from the station; accommodates about 20; $1.50 per day, $7 per week, $20 per month and upward.
Branch House. Mrs. A. S. Branch, Proprietor. Three hundred yards from the station; accommodates 20; $1.50 per day, $7 per week, $20 per month and upward.

Sutherland, Hillsboro Co., Florida.—On the Gulf of Mexico, and also a station on the Orange Belt Ry.; population of the community about 200; telegraph and Southern Express Co.'s office; ample facilities for boating, fishing, and hunting.
O. Tinney, Agent, Orange Belt Ry.
Gulf View.—C. T. Taylor, Omaha, Nebraska, Proprietor; Briard F. Hill, Manager. One block from the station; accommodates 200; $2 to $4 per day, $12 to $25 per week.
Hotel San Marino.—Dr. H. V. Coffman, Omaha, Nebraska, Proprietor; Briard F. Hill, Manager. Four blocks from the station; accommodates 200; $2 to $4 per day, $12 to $25 per week.

Suwanee, Suwanee Co., Florida.—Station on the S., F. & W. Ry., direct from Savannah; population of the community, 200; 7 miles from Live Oak; the location of one of the largest sulphur springs; a great health resort, in both summer and winter; spring flows 45,000 gallons per minute; telegraph and Southern Express Co.'s office.
Suwanee Sulphur Springs Hotel.—S. H. Peck, Proprietor. One mile from the station by street car; accommodates 200; $2.50 to $4 per day, $15 to $21 per week, $60 to $70 per month.

THE SAVANNAH LINE IS PREPARED TO

Suwanee River.—This river, being celebrated in song, must not be omitted.

> "Away down on the Suwanee River,
> Far, far away,
> There's where my heart is turning ever;
> There's where the old folks stay."

One of the largest rivers south-east of the Mississippi, empties into the Gulf of Mexico 12 miles north-west of Cedar Key. Steamers make regular trips on this river between Cedar Key and Luraville from the islands of the Cedar Key group, in the Gulf, to the head of navigation, connecting with the F. C. & P. Ry. at Cedar Key, and the S., F. & W. at Branford. The scenery is beautiful.

J. O. Andrews, General Passenger Agent, Cedar Key, Florida, will cheerfully give information.

Suwanee Shoals, Columbia Co., Florida.—Four miles from White Springs, 10 miles from Lake City; population of the community, 150.

P. G. Brown will give information.

Sycamore, Gadsden Co., Florida.—Fourteen miles from Quincy.

Sylacauga, Talladega Co., Georgia.—Station on the S. & W. Division of Central R. R. of Georgia; population, 950; money-order, telegraph, and Southern Express Co.'s office; mining industries—stone, marble, iron, slate, &c.

C. A. Walker, Agent, C. R. R. of Georgia.
Sylacauga Inn.—A. V. Levejing, Proprietor. Five hundred yards from the station by hack; accommodates 200; $2 per day, $10 per week, $40 per month.
Meachem House.—W. C. Meachem, Proprietor. Accommodates 100; $2 per day, $10 per week, $30 per month.

Sylvan Lake, Orange Co., Florida.—Station on the Orange Belt Ry., 6 miles from Sanford; population of the community about 100; good fishing, hunting, and driving; in the midst of pine woods, dotted with lakes and bearing orange groves.

Thomas E. Wilson or W. R. Robbins will give information.
Villa Clare.—Mrs. G. W. Davis, Proprietor. Accommodates 40; $1 to $2 per day, $5 to $10 per week, special by the month.
Orange View or Warren House.—Josiah Warren, Proprietor. Accommodates 40; $1 to $2 per day, $5 to $10 per week, special by the month.

Tallahassee, Leon Co., Florida.—Capital of the State; on the Western Division of the F. C. & P. R. R.; population, 4000; situated among high hills, rolling lands; good roads; Wakulla Crystal Springs; water so clear the objects are plainly visible at great depth; Newport Springs; St. Mark's and light-house; all easy of access.

J. T. Bernard & Son will give information.
The "Leon."—M. L. Oglesby, Manager. (Summer address, Buffalo Lithia Springs, Va.) First class in every respect; accommodates 200; $3 to $4 per day, $18 to $28 per week.
St. James Hotel.—G. A. Lamb, Manager. Accommodates 100; $2.50 to $3.50 per day, special by the week or month.

HANDLE FREIGHT MORE PROMPTLY THAN OTHERS.

THE PLANT SYSTEM

AND STEAMSHIP LINES.

Tampa, Hillsboro Co., Florida.—At the head of Tampa Bay, and at the mouth of the Hillsboro River; terminus of the main line of the South Florida R. R. and the Tampa Division of the F. C. & P. R. R.; population, 10,000; has all the conveniences of a city,—gas, water, electric lights, and street cars,—and is a bustling city; in its north portion (Ybor City) are located numerous large cigar factories, employing thousands of Cuban cigar makers, who form quite a settlement in that locality. Tampa has one of the finest hotels (The Tampa Bay) in the world. Port Tampa, the greatest shipping port on the Gulf, is only 9 miles distant (see Port Tampa) by frequent trains. Fishing, hunting, boating, sailing, and driving.

Tampa is of interest historically, being the place where Ferdinand De Soto landed May 25th, 1539. From there he started on his search for the mines of wealth supposed to exist in the New World, which resulted in the discovery of the Mississippi River. From there also Narvaez, having obtained a grant of Florida from Charles V. of Spain, landed with a large force April 16th, 1528.

J. A. M. Grable, Agent, South Florida R. R., or **John S. McFall**, Freight Agent, or **J. A. White**, Ticket Agent, F. C. & P. R. R., will give information.

Tampa Bay Hotel.—Tampa Bay Hotel Co., Proprietor. J. H. King, Manager. South Florida R. R. trains land passengers at the door; over 500 feet long, with walls of brick and beams of steel, arched with concrete and floored with tiles, proof against any fire; massive, yet light and graceful in its perfect Moorish architecture; with colonnades, porches, and balconies looking out through 100 beautiful arches upon as many pictures; minarets, domes, and pinnacles rising 150 feet above the lawns that gently slope away in front, and fall, with green terraces, to the water's edge. Sheltered promenades among the towers that overlook a park of 150 acres of groves, avenues, gardens, fountains, bridges, and waterways; with mineral springs of famous qualities; floats and pavilion for boats and launches; drives, walks, and bathing beaches, and the town beyond, and the coming and going trains. With parlor and music, and dining halls rich in every appointment; apartments *en suite*, with every comfort of a private mansion; baths, electric lights, and luxury everywhere,—the whole interior being fitted with the very latest improvements that science and art can contribute; while the decorations, furniture, and effects are prepared with the broadest range of diversity that good taste and judgment can dictate; a veritable palace and home. $5 per day and upward.

The Almeria.—E. S. Douglass, Proprietor. Accommodates 200; $4 per day, $25 per week and upward.

The Plant.—B. R. Cole, Proprietor. Accommodates 100; $2 per day and upward, special by the week or month.

Palmetto Hotel.—R. F. Webb, Proprietor. Accommodates 60; $2 per day and upward, special by the week or month.

Gulf House.—J. W. Booz, Proprietor. Accommodates 50; $2 per day and upward, special by the week or month.

Ample accommodations in other hotels and private boarding-houses and furnished apartments, at rates of $6 per week and upward.

Tangerine, Orange Co., Florida.—Two and one-half miles from Mount Dora; high, rolling pine lands; beautiful lake; good hunting and fishing.

William H. Earle will give information.

Wachusett Hotel.—William H. Earle, Proprietor. Accommodates 50; $2 per day, $7 to $9 per week; summer address, Worcester, Mass.; will meet train with team.

THE SAVANNAH LINE STEAMERS ARE THE FINEST.

Tarpon Springs, Hillsboro Co., Florida.—Station on the Orange Belt Ry.; population, 700; money-order, telegraph, and Southern Express Co.'s offices; very attractive spot near the Gulf: fishing, sailing, and boating; many pleasure steam and naphtha launches; sail boats, &c.
J. Patten or Merrick Whitcomb will give information.
Tarpon Springs Hotel.—Tarpon Springs I. & D. Co. (1233 Filbert Street, Philadelphia, Pa.) Proprietors; A. P. Weller, Resident Superintendent. Accommodates 150; $2.50 to $4 per day, special by the week or month.
Besides the above there are, "**The Tropical,**" **Russell House, Fernald Cottage,** and several private boarding-houses.

Tavares, Lake Co., Florida.—A station on the Florida Southern Ry. and the S. & L. E. Divisions of the J., T. & K. W. system; on the Southern Division of the F. C. & P. R. R.; on Tavares & Gulf R. R.; population of the community, 300; money-order, telegraph, and Southern Express Co.'s offices; good hunting, fishing, and boating; several large lakes near by.
E. S. Johnson, Freight and Ticket Agent, J., T. & K. W. system, or R. T. Way, Freight Agent, and G W. Terry, Ticket Agent, F. C. & P. R. R., will give information.
Osceola Hotel.—Frank Jones, Owner; C. L. York, Manager. Accommodates 100; $2.50 to $3 per day, special by the week or month.

Tennille, Washington Co., Georgia.—Station on the main stem of the C. R. R. of Georgia; population, 1000; money-order, telegraph, and Southern Express Co.'s offices.
W. C. Matthews, Agent, C. R. R. of Ga.

Thomaston, Upson Co., Georgia.—On the main stem of the Central R. R. of Georgia; population, 2000; money-order, telegraph, and Southern Express Co.'s offices; mineral springs of noted medical qualities.
A. W. White, Agent, C. R. R. of Ga.
Chenny House.—J. C. McCrory, Proprietor. Accommodates 50; $3 per day, $18 per week; near the station.
Numerous private boarding-houses at $10 per month and upward.

Thomasville, Thomas Co., Georgia.—On the S.. F. & W. Ry. direct from Savannah; a well-known winter resort; population, 6000; all the conveniences of a modern city; fine drives: good hunting and fishing; has churches of all denominations; large opera house.
Address F. M. Van Dyke, Ticket Agent, S., F. & W. Ry., or H. W. Hopkins or E. M. Mallette, for information.
Piney Woods Hotel.—M. A. Bower, Owner; Wm. E. Davies, Manager. Accommodates 300; with all the conveniences and attachments of any first-class hotel; $4 per day, $25 per week.
Mitchell House.
The Masury.
Clarendon.—S. B. Van Dyke, Proprietor. Accommodates 50; $2 per day and upward, special by the week or month.
Stuart's Hotel.—C. T. Stuart, Proprietor. Accommodates 175; $2 to $2.50 per day, $10 to $14 per week, $40 to $50 per month.
Hotel Brighton.—Miller & Co., Proprietors. Accommodates 70 (on European plan); rooms $1 per day, $7 per week, $30 per month.
Scott House.
Pine Summit.
Uhler House.
Numerous private boarding-houses, at rates of $6 per week and upward.

ALWAYS TRAVEL VIA THE SAVANNAH LINE.

Thompson, Bullock Co., Alabama.—Station on the South-western Division of the C. R. R. of Georgia; population, 250.
  B. L. Perry, Agent, C. R. R. of Georgia.

Thonotosassa, Hillsboro Co., Florida.—Six miles from Seffner, on Lake Thonotosassa; population of the community, 400; good boating and fishing; fine orange section.
  Grand View House.—E. E. Hazen, Proprietor. Accommodates 20; $2 per day, $6 to $8 per week.
  E. E. Hazen will give information.

Three Notch, Bullock Co., Alabama.—Station on the South-western Division of the C. R. R. of Georgia.
  J. W. Bledsoe, Agent, C. R. R. of Georgia.

Titusville, Brevard Co., Florida.—On the Indian River; junction of the J., T. & K. W. Ry. with Indian River steamers; population, 1000; money-order, telegraph, and Southern Express Co.'s offices; good fishing, sailing, and boating on the Indian River; good hunting; numerous orange groves.
  M. E. Gruber, Agent, J., T. & K. W. Ry.
  Indian River Hotel.—J. M. Mabbette, Proprietor. Accommodates 125; $2 to $3.50 per day, special by the week or month.
  Grand View Hotel.—J. M. Mabbette, Proprietor. Accommodates 75; $2 per day, special by the week or month.

Tropic, Brevard Co., Florida.—On the Indian River; fishing, hunting, and boating; pineapples and tropical fruits and flowers.
  The Casper House.—J. L. Casper, Proprietor. Accommodates 15; $2 per day, $10 per week, $30 per month.

Twin Lakes, Pasco Co., Florida.—Twelve miles from Dade City; 3 beautiful lakes; orange groves; good hunting and fishing.
  John H. Reilley will give information.

Umatilla, Lake Co., Florida.—On the Florida Southern Ry. Division of the J., T. & K. W. system, 21 miles from Astor, 18 miles from Leesburg; large acreage in vegetables; oranges, lemons, &c.; numerous clear-water lakes; good hunting and fishing.
  John A. Mitchener will give information.
  Umatilla House.—J. A. Mitchener, Proprietor. Accommodates 75; $2 per day, $6 to $8 per week, $20 to $25 per month.

Upsala (or New Upsala), Orange Co., Florida.—Station on the S. & L. E. Division of the J., T. & K. W. Ry., 3 miles from Sanford; numerous orange groves.
  B. O. Seltzer will give information.

Valdosta, Lowndes Co., Georgia.—Station on the S., F. & W. Ry., direct from Savannah; population, 3000; money-order, telegraph, and Southern Express Co.'s offices.
  Stuart House.—Mrs. B. F. Moseley, Proprietor; J. H. Stump, Manager. Accommodates 75; $2 per day, $10 per week, $30 per month.

Southern Products Transported Promptly.

Vernon, Washington Co., Florida.—Sixteen miles from Chipley.

Viana, Citrus Co., Florida.—Four miles west of Hernando.

Victoria, Lake Co., Florida.—Station on the Southern Division of the F. C. & P. R. R., 6 miles from Zellwood; good fishing and hunting; abundance of quail.
J. L. Lavake will give information.

Villa City, Lake Co., Florida.—Three miles from Mascotte; population of the community, 350; beautiful locality; clear-water lakes; good orange and vegetable section; rolling lands; good hunting and fishing.
Geo. T. King will give information.
Fern Villa.—Mrs. A. Gall, Proprietor. Summer address, Ocean Grove, N. J. Public carriage from station; accommodates 50; $2 per day, $12 per week, $45 per month.

Viola, Lake Co., Florida.—On Lake Griffin; 10 miles from Leesburg by daily steamer; good fishing; large or small game for hunters; numerous bearing orange groves.
M. C. Sligh will give information.
The Lake View.—M. C. Sligh, Proprietor. Accommodates 12; $1 per day, $5 per week, $20 per month.

Wadley, Jefferson Co., Georgia. On the main stem of the C. R. R. of Georgia; population, 1000; money-order, telegraph, and Southern Express Company's offices.
H. H. Woodruff, Agent, C. R. R. of Georgia.
Terminal Hotel.—W. E. Taylor, Proprietor. Accommodates 75; $2 per day, special by the week or month.
Donovan House. T. J. Shivers, Proprietor. Accommodates 40; $2 per day, special by the week or month.

Wahneta, Polk Co., Florida.—(Post-office name for Bartow Junction.)

Waldo, Alachua Co., Florida.—Junction of the Southern and Cedar Key Divisions of the F. C. & P. R. R.; population, 700; money-order, telegraph, and Southern Express Company's offices; 2 fine lakes near by, affording good fishing and boating; plenty of large game for huntsmen's sport.
V. H. Bell, Agent, F. C. & P. R. R., or J. C. Deane, will give information.
Waldo House.—Fred Willor, Proprietor. Accommodates 100; $2 per day, $10 per week.
Renault House.—E. Renault, Proprietor. Accommodates 35; $2 per day, special by the week or month.

Watertown, Columbia Co., Florida.—Station on the Western Division of the F. C. & P. R. R., 3 miles from Lake City.
Thomas Dowling, Agent, F. C. & P. R. R., will give information.

Wauchula, De Soto Co., Florida. Station on the Charlotte Harbor Division of the Florida Southern Ry., near Peace River; population of the community, 300; money-order, telegraph, and Southern Express Co.'s offices.
A. G. Smith, Agent, or M. A. Payne will give information.
Wauchula House. M. A. Payne, Proprietor. Accommodates 20; $2 per day, $5 per week.

UNEQUALED FACILITIES.

Waycross, Ware Co., Georgia.—Junction of the S., F. & W. and B. & W. Rys.; "The Funnel," through which all business passes into Florida; population, 4000; live, pushing city.

A. M. Knight, Mayor, will give information.
Strickland House.—J. W. Strickland, Proprietor. Accommodates 35; $2 per day, special by the week or month.
Phœnix.—W. Stewart, Proprietor. Accommodates 100; $2 to $3 per day, special by the week or month.
Weiss House.—Mrs. J. Weiss, Proprietor. Accommodates 50; $2 to $3 per day, special by the week or month.

Webster, Sumter Co., Florida.—Station on the Florida Southern Ry. Division of the J., T. & K. W. system; population, 800; telegraph and Southern Express Co.'s office; fishing, hunting, deer, turkey, and small game.

J. W. Sheppard, Agent, Florida Southern Ry., will give information.
Arnold House.—William Arnold, Proprietor. $2 per day, $10 per week.
Private board at $1.50 per day, $12 to $20 per month.

Weir Park, Marion Co., Florida.—Station on the Florida Southern Ry. Division of the J., T. & K. W. system, also landing on Lake Weir; telegraph and Southern Express Co.'s offices; fine hunting, fishing, and boating; fine orange groves.

J. H. Carter, Agent, Florida Southern Ry.
Weir Park Hotel.—R. L. Martin, Proprietor. Accommodates 30; $2 per day, $9 per week, $30 per month.

Welaka, Putnam Co., Florida.—Landing on the east bank of the St. John's River, opposite mouth of the Ocklawaha River; 4½ miles from Sisco; good fishing; sulphur springs for bathing.

F. E. Reeder will give information.
Reeder House.—F. E. Reeder, Proprietor. Near the landing; $1.75 per day, $10 per week, $38 per month.

Welshton, Marion Co., Florida.—Station on the Florida Southern Ry. Division of the J., T. & K. W. system; population of the community, 600; money-order, telegraph, and Southern Express Co.'s offices.

J. H. Welsh, Agent, Florida Southern Ry., will give information.

West Farm, Madison Co., Florida.—Station on the Western Division of the F. C. & P. R. R., 5 miles from Madison; population of the community, 300; Southern Express Company's office.

J. G. Blackwell, Agent, F. C. & P. R. R., will give information.
Blackwell Hotel.—Mrs. Bettie Lee, Proprietor. Accommodates 25; $1 per day, $4 to $6 per week, $15 to $20 per month.

Wetappo, Washington Co., Florida.—At the east end of St. Andrew's Bay; 80 miles by boat from St. Andrew's; 80 miles from Chipley.
Dr. J. W. Keyes will give information.

Wewahitchka, Calhoun Co., Florida.—On the Chipola River; Barnesville, Georgia, nearest railroad station; fishing and hunting.

Wewahitchka R. E. & I. Co. will give information.
The Castle.—S. S. Alderman, Proprietor. Accommodates 50; $1.50 per day.
E. Z. Taylor.—Private board. $1 per day.

THE SAVANNAH LINE STEAMERS ARE THE FINEST.

Whitesburg, Carroll Co., Georgia.—Station on the Savannah & Western Division of the C. R. R. of Georgia; population, 400; money-order, telegraph, and Southern Express Company's offices; good farming section; good schools; 2 churches; no saloons; grapes being grown successfully.

Messrs. Almon & Gordon will give information.
Harris House.—Mrs. M. T. Harris, Proprietor. Accommodates 10; $2 per day, $5 per week, $12.50 per month.

White Springs, Hamilton Co., Florida.—On the G. S. & F. R. R. and on the Suwanee River; population, 500; telegraph and Southern Express Company's offices; fine mineral spring; plunge and swimming pool; good hunting; fishing and boating on the Suwanee River.

C. L. Morrison will give information.
White Springs Hotel.—G. A. Wright, Owner; W. T. King, Manager. Accommodates 150; $2 per day, $10 per week, $35 per month.

Whitney, Lake Co., Florida.—Station on the Southern Division of the F. C. & P. R. R., 4 miles from Leesburg; good pine and hammock lands.

E. J. Merrilus will give information.

Wilderness (P. O. name Belmore), Clay Co., Florida.—On the Western Ry. of Florida; in the midst of good fruit and vegetable lands; good hunting.

T. H. Jarvis will give information.
Wilson House.—Lewis Wilson, Proprietor.

Wildwood, Sumter Co., Florida.—Junction of the Southern and Tampa Divisions of the F. C. & P. R. R.; population of the community, 800; money-order, telegraph, and Southern Express Co.'s offices; located at the head of Gulf Hammock; one of the finest places for game, both large and small.

J. T. Bryan, Agent, F. C. & P. R. R., will give information.
Withlacoochee Hotel.—J. E. Barwick, Owner; Miss Annie Barwick, Manager. Accommodates 50; $2 per day, $5 to $10 per week, $20 to $30 per month.
Wildwood Hotel.—D. H. Hart, Proprietor. Accommodates 40; $2 per day, $5 to $10 per week, $20 to $30 per month.

Williston, Levy Co., Florida.—Eleven miles from Archer; in the midst of good phosphate and timber lands.

J. B. Epperson will give information.
Private board by J. B. Epperson. Accommodates 10; $1.50 per day, special by the week or month.

Willow, Hillsboro Co., Florida.—At the head of navigation, on Little Manatee River, 13 miles from Brantley.

C. B. Hester will give information.

Winter Haven, Polk Co., Florida.—Station on the Bartow Branch of the South Florida R. R.; money-order, telegraph, and Southern Express Co.'s offices; high, rolling pine land; attractive scenery; over 25 clear-water lakes within a radius of 2 miles.

R. H. Peacock will give information.
Clayton House.—J. B. Clayton, Proprietor. Accommodates 25; $1.50 per day, $7 per week.

TICKETS INCLUDE MEALS AND BERTH.

Winter Park, Orange Co., Florida.—On the main line of the South Florida R. R., and also on the E. F. & A. R. R.; population of the community, 800; money-order, telegraph, and Southern Express Co.'s office; one of the finest winter resorts in the State; numerous fine winter residences; many beautiful clear-water lakes; 12 lakes can be seen from observatory on hotel; ample supply of small pleasure craft on the lake; steam launches; seat of Rollins College, a first-class educational institution, amply endowed; good boating, fishing, and hunting.

E. A. Faulkner, Agent, South Florida R. R.
J. S. Capen or Charles J. Ladd will give information.
The Seminole.—Plant Investment Co., Owners. F. C. Campbell, Manager. Horse cars from station; accommodates 500; $4 per day and upward, special by the week or month; first class in every respect, with telegraph service, livery, and pleasure boats.
The Rogers House.—A. E. & A. R. Rogers, Proprietors. Accommodates 80; $2 to $3 per day, $10 to $18 per week.
Osceola House.—W. J. Waddell, Proprietor. Accommodates 35; $2 per day $10 to $12 per week.
Palmetto House.—J. D. Taylor, Proprietor. Accommodates 40; $1.50 per day, $8 per week, $20 per month.

Woodbridge (or Mayo), Orange Co., Florida.—Station on the main line of the South Florida R. R., near Maitland.

Wyrtle, Montgomery Co., Alabama.—(P. O. name for **Perry's Mills,** Alabama.)

York, Marion Co., Florida.—Two miles from Leroy; population, 100.

Zellwood, Orange Co., Florida.—Station on the Southern Division of the F. C. & P. R. R., 8 miles from Apopka; population of the community, 500; high, rolling country; many beautiful clear-water lakes; many winter homes here.

M. E. Barnes, Agent, F. C. & P. R. R., or D. H. Fleming will give information.
The Mitchellhurst.—Mrs. M. D. Mitchell, Proprietor Summer address, Philadelphia, Pa. Accommodates 25; $1.50 to $3 per day, $10 to $15 per week, $25 to $40 per month.
Scott Cottage.—Mrs. C. H. Scott, Proprietor. Accommodates 15; $1.50 to $2 per day, $10 to $15 per week, $25 to $40 per month.

Zolfo Springs, De Soto Co., Florida.—Flag station on the Charlotte Harbor Division of the Florida Southern Ry.

THE PLANT SYSTEM OF RAILWAY AND STEAMSHIP LINES.

HUNTING IN GEORGIA.

There is no general or State law governing the hunting season, and the several local or county laws on the subject are not uniform as to dates of opening and closing. More attention is paid to such matters on the seaboard than elsewhere; and in the neighborhood of Savannah and counties adjacent the season for deer, partridges, wild turkeys, ducks, &c. opens October 1st, and closes April 1st following. From April to October hunting is prohibited.

HUNTING IN FLORIDA.

The following are the salient points of the Game Laws of Florida, as recently enacted and now in force:—

No person shall chase or kill wild deer, in any part of the State, for more than four months in any year. The boards of county commissioners shall indicate the opening and closing of the season in their several counties. Should the commissioners in any county fail to designate the hunting period the same shall be in each county during the months of November, December, January, and February. No person shall hunt or kill any wild turkey, quail, or partridge, in any part of this State, save only from the first day of November until the first day of March.

THE SAVANNAH LINE STEAMERS ARE THE FINEST.

ALWAYS TRAVEL BY THE SAVANNAH LINE

www.ingramcontent.com/pod-product-compliance
Lightning Source LLC
Chambersburg PA
CBHW020129170426
43199CB00010B/696